The Importance of Covering

The Importance of Covering

Lance Lambert

LANCE LAMBERT MINISTRIES
Richmond, VA

ISBN: 978-1-68389-074-4
www.lancelambert.org

Contents

Preface

This series of messages on covering was given by Lance Lambert in 1971 at Halford House in Richmond, Surrey. His spoken words have been transcribed into this book and edited only for clarity.

As shared by Lance Lambert, covering is perhaps one of the most vitally important subjects that God's people could study. In this series, he shows that this matter of covering, or being hid, is one of the strong emphases of the Bible from its beginning to its end.

He that dwelleth in the secret place of the Most High shall abide under the shadow of the Almighty. Psalm 91:1

For those who abide in God, who dwelleth in the secret place, the covered place, the Almighty is their protection, their security, their safety. The Almighty will come between them and anything hostile.

As the days grow evil and the world tries to devour the Lord's people, it is vital that we come under and stay under the covering of our God, that we boldly enter the holy place by the blood of Jesus.

1.
Survey in the Old Testament

Psalm 91

He that dwelleth in the secret place of the Most High, shall abide under the shadow of the Almighty. I will say of the Lord, He is my refuge and my fortress; My God, in whom I trust. For he will deliver thee from the snare of the fowler, and from the deadly pestilence. He will cover thee with his pinions, and under his wings shalt thou take refuge: His truth is a shield and a buckler. Thou shalt not be afraid for the terror by night, nor for the arrow that flieth by day; For the pestilence that walketh in darkness, Nor for the destruction that wasteth at noonday. A thousand shall fall at thy side, and ten thousand at thy right hand; But it shall not come nigh thee. Only with thine eyes shalt thou behold, and see the reward of the wicked. For thou, O Lord, art my refuge! Thou hast made the Most High thy habitation; There shall no evil befall thee, neither shall any plague come nigh thy tent. For he will give his angels charge over thee, to keep thee in all thy ways. They shall bear thee up in their hands, lest thou dash thy foot against a stone. Thou shalt tread upon the lion and adder: the young lion and the serpent shalt thou trample under foot. Because he hath set his love upon me, therefore will I deliver him: I will set him on high, because he hath known my name. He shall call upon me, and I will answer him; I will be with him in trouble; I will deliver him, and honor him. With long life will I satisfy him, and show him my salvation.

Ephesians 6:10–20

Finally, be strong in the Lord, and in the strength of his might. Put on the whole armor of God, that ye may be able to stand against the wiles of the devil. For our wrestling is not against flesh and blood, but against the principalities, against the powers, against the world-rulers of this darkness, against the spiritual hosts of wickedness in the heavenly places. Wherefore take up the whole armor of God, that ye may be able to withstand in the evil day, and having done all, to stand. Stand therefore, having girded your loins with truth, and having put on the breastplate of righteousness, and having shod your feet with the preparation of the gospel of peace; withal taking up the shield of faith, wherewith ye shall be able to quench all the fiery darts of the evil one. And take the helmet of salvation, and the sword of the Spirit, which is the word of God: with all prayer and supplication praying at all seasons in the Spirit, and watching thereunto in all perseverance and supplication for all the saints, and on my behalf, that utterance may be given unto me in opening my mouth, to

make known with boldness the mystery of the gospel, for which I am an ambassador in chains;	*that in it I may speak boldly, as I ought to speak.*

Shall we pray?

Dear Lord, we thank Thee Thou art with us. Thou knowest we are all different ages, spiritually, different conditions, different backgrounds. Oh Father, we pray, by Thy Spirit, take this subject and bring it in life to every one of us, and may something of its importance dawn upon us. We ask it in His name. Amen.

The subject we are considering is covering. It is perhaps one of the most vitally important subjects that we could study. I have no doubt that there are some who might say, "I have never heard of covering. Where does it speak of covering in the Bible?" The fact is that this matter of covering, or being hid, is one of the strong emphases of the Bible from its beginning to its end. It is summed up in that wonderful Psalm 91 which is really a continuation of Psalm 90. It is the same Psalm, but it was divided into two. You will notice that in Psalm 90:1, it says, "Lord, thou hast been our dwelling place in all generations."

Then, in Psalm 91:1, it says, "He that dwelleth in the secret place of the Most High shall abide under the shadow of the Almighty." Perhaps you have never thought of that as covering, but that is exactly what it is. "He that dwelleth in the secret place (the covert, the secret place, the covered place) of the Most High shall abide (shall remain) under the shadow of the Almighty." The Almighty will be his protection; the Almighty will be his security; the Almighty will be his safety; the Almighty will come between him and anything hostile. "He that has made the Lord his habitation; he that dwells in the secret place of the Most High."

Protection from Hostile Things

This Psalm speaks about all kinds of terrors. It speaks of the terrors of the night, horrors of the night. It speaks of pestilence, which is not only physical pestilence, but spiritual pestilence too. Many, many Christians suffer from spiritual pestilence–disease, some infection that won't clear up that is just getting them down all the time. Sometimes they think it is just something to do with the way that they are meant to walk; but it is not. It is because they have become uncovered. The Word of God says here quite clearly that the pestilence or the plague shall not come. "He shall not be afraid of the pestilence that walketh in darkness nor for the destruction that wasteth at noonday" (v.6).

If you know anything about the East, you know there is a kind of plague, a kind of disease, a kind of infection, which can sweep through a community within hours and decimate it. That is really what the Psalmist is speaking of here a pestilence of "a destruction that wasteth at noonday" that lays everything low, suddenly, almost without explanation. He speaks of a plague coming nigh your tent–"It shall not come nigh your tent." He speaks of war–"A thousand falling at your side, ten thousand at your right hand but it shall not come nigh thee."

The whole Psalm speaks of all kinds of hostile things: things that would come out against the child of God; things that would come out against the church of God to destroy it. But that is not the emphasis of this Psalm. It is not that the Christian is surrounded by hostility, that the Christian ought to be frightened to death by all the things that are around him. The whole emphasis of this Psalm is covering. The child of God can walk with his head high in the air; the child of God can have boldness to come into the most holy place of all by the blood of Jesus, by that new and living way which is Christ, Himself. That is the emphasis of this Psalm.

If you come out from under covering, immediately hostile forces can get their grip on you. If you keep under covering, you are safe. There is no matter more important to both young and old believers than this matter. When I am asked what I think is one of the most essential things for a young believer to know, I would say straightaway, "How to be covered and how to remain covered as a child of God." If an older believer says to me, "What do you think is the most important thing I should know?", I would say straightaway, "How to be covered." I have seen quite a number of people go off the rails. It all began with uncovering. There is a stupidity about many of us, an arrogance, a presumption, an insensitivity to the things of God and to the ways of God. Sometimes, we see His acts and we do not understand His ways; but because of that, we are undone in the end. Pride always goes before a fall. But to be proud you don't have to be haughty in your dealings with other people. You can be haughty in your dealings with God as if God should open everything up to you; or as if you have a right to tell God what to do in a kind of arrogant and presumptuous way. That is the pride that goes before a fall, and that is the kind of thing we are talking about.

The Enemy's Objective

I know some great servants of the Lord who, in their last days, got uncovered. The enemy has a great objective with every single child of God and with the church of God; it is to get us uncovered. He cannot do anything when the church of God is covered. There is not a single thing Satan can do with the church unless it is permitted and allowed by God. Therefore, the enemy's whole plan, his design, his objective, his strategy in this war is to push the church out from covering, to get it exposed and to get it out into the open, away from its safety. Then the enemy can come and demolish it. His strategy is exactly the same with the child of God. His whole strategy is to push the child of God into a position where that one comes out from under covering. He tries to meet the enemy himself or herself, and the enemy knows exactly what to do with the very best of us.

Later, we shall be dealing with some great examples in the Old Testament and then the New; but for now I think immediately of David. He got uncovered when he didn't go out to war with his men. He was not at the head where he should have been. He stayed back, and he was uncovered. While he was in that position, perhaps he thought to himself, "I will read the Scriptures. I will have a wonderful time of mediation and reflection." He went up on his rooftop to have this meditation and reflection, but he was uncovered. (We can even talk about spiritual things and yet be uncovered, if we are out of the will of God.) There he saw

Bathsheba, and the whole foul idea of murdering her husband and taking her took root in his heart. Where did such a foul and vile idea originate if it did not originate in Satan? He was out to destroy David and the whole work of God in the people of God. It is a wonderful thing that God understood who was behind it all, and it is a wonderful thing that David finally got back under covering and said:

Blessed is he whose transgression is forgiven,
whose sin is covered. Psalm 32:1

In his great letter to the church at Ephesus, which I think all of us agree is the high water mark of revelation in the New Testament, the Apostle Paul comes right back to this whole matter of covering in his final word. You may not think of it as covering, but that is exactly what it is: "Wherefore put on the whole armor of God." Don't leave a single chink from head to foot; be covered. There is something of Christ for every part of your being. It is very interesting that, really, he is not just speaking of individuals there, but he is speaking to the whole church. He is saying to you all: "Put on the armor of God together. See that Christ is the helmet, that He is the breastplate, that He is the girdle or the belt, that He is the shoes on your feet, that He is the shield of faith, that He is the sword in your hand." That is covering.

The apostle knew very well that no company of believers who begins to see something of the eternal purpose of God, nor any child of God who begins to see something more than forgiveness of sins, who begins to see that behind it all lies a tremendous purpose from eternity to eternity, is safe unless he knows how to put on the whole armor of God. Our trouble on this matter of covering is that we all go by these eyes and by our physical senses. It is like being exposed to invisible rays. If there is something radioactive in a room, no one in the room can see the rays, no one can see the danger; but every single person will be exposed to death-giving rays. All will be exposed to something. That is what this whole matter of covering is about. Spiritually, we can be exposed to things that we cannot see or sense with our physical senses, but which we can know about if we have our spiritual senses exercised. We can know things that are coming at us. The whole problem is one of covering. If you are covered, none of those dangerous or injurious things can harm you.

I remember as a little boy at the time of the war, I was always mystified by all those old gentlemen going to work with umbrellas and helmets. I could not understand what those helmets were when I was a little boy, but I was told it was something to do with shrapnel. Just recently in Belfast, a young lad lost his life as he leaned out of a sentry tower to speak with his relief. He had not put on his protective vest and a bullet got him. That is what covering is: never to be without your protective vest, spiritually; never to be without that helmet of salvation, spiritually; always having on the armor of God.

The temptation of Christ was just along this line. There were three main ways that Satan tempted or tried the Lord Jesus, and each time he used Scripture. What was Satan trying to do? We know that the Lord Jesus could easily have turned stones into bread. After all, a little later on in His life, He did feed over five thousand people with five loaves and two fish; and on another occasion, He fed four thousand people with seven loaves and a few fish. He could easily have done this; why didn't He? Wouldn't it have silenced the devil if the Lord Jesus had just commanded that these stones be made bread? But the whole point was this: the Lord Jesus was being tried not as God but as Man. He knew in His heart that He had no direction from God to turn those stones into bread. The devil's whole objective was to get Him to act independently of God; to get Him to do something which seemed to be right and legitimate, that expressed faith and was a miracle of the first order, but was done apart from God. If the Lord Jesus had done that, immediately, He would have been exposed to enemy interference.

Then, the devil took Him upon a high pinnacle of the temple and said, "Cast yourself down." He quoted the very Scripture from Psalm 91: "He shall give His angels charge concerning thee. On their hands they shall bear thee up, lest haply thou dash thy foot against a stone." This is the Psalm about covering we have been considering. Wouldn't it have been an easy thing for the Lord Jesus just to have done it? Many times when they were going to lynch Him, He walked straight through them; not a man could touch Him. It would have been an easy thing for Him and a rather wonderful thing. The devil knew very well that Christ could turn stones into bread, and he knew very well that the Lord Jesus could come down from the highest pinnacle of the temple and come down safely. He knew it! Satan wanted to force the Lord Jesus to act apart from His Father.

If he could only do that, he would expose Him to the deadly rays from another world. So you can go through these temptations and see it is all to do with this matter of covering.

I cannot profess to understand fully this subject; and therefore, I want to say to you that I am as much a student in this as anyone else. What I know is that we are touching something like an iceberg; very little is above the surface. The vast amount of this whole matter lies hidden underneath. Therefore, all I can do is whet your appetite, point out a number of things, put a question mark over some of them, and explain a few others as far as I am able. If, as a result of this ministry, the fear of the Lord comes upon us, it has been well worthwhile.

The Fear of the Lord

Where is the fear of the Lord today among the people of God? I have seen people die under the hand of God. I have seen that the Lord is still the living God. You cannot play about with Him. He is like a consuming fire. He must be treated with awe and reverence. Now I am not asking for that cringing kind of fear that some people associate with the fear of the Lord; nor am I asking that people should suddenly all become frightened to do anything, frightened to say anything, frightened to contribute because of the Lord. That is not the fear of the Lord. At the time of Pentecost, when the church was strongest and the authority of the Lord was most manifest, the fear of the Lord came upon those people again and again and again.

Great fear fell upon the whole church. Acts 2:43

What did it mean? It did not stop them from contributing; it did not stop them from witnessing; it did not stop them from working;

it did not stop the Lord from manifesting Himself in and through them; but there was great fear upon them all. Oh, to be done with this nonsensical stuff that sometimes goes for the work of the Spirit. It is nothing but the soul in the realm of the spirit. When the Spirit of God really starts to work, a reverence comes upon us and an awe comes upon us. We begin to watch the way we dress; we begin to watch the way we conduct ourselves; we begin to watch the way that we behave because we know with whom we have to do. We love Him. It is not a cringing fear with torment and punishment; from that we must be delivered. But it is a kind of fear which comes out of a sensitive love for God.

The fear of the Lord is something we do not find in the twentieth century. We associate it with the Dark Ages or the Middle Ages, but God has not changed. The twentieth century does not mean that God's power is less or that He is less of a consuming fire than He ever was. God does not change. God is the same, always the same.

Jesus Christ is the same yesterday, today
and forever. Hebrews 13:8

Therefore, I hope that in touching this whole matter, if nothing else, the profundity of it, the mystery of it will so come upon us, that an inquiring and sensitive spirit may be produced in us all in our walk with God.

Old Testament References

Personal

We are going to look at some of the various references to covering in the Old Testament. We cannot look at all of them, but a lot of them. First of all, we will go on a few circuits; and the first circuit is a personal one.

> *And the Lord said, Behold, there is a place by me, and thou*
> *shalt stand upon the rock: and it shall come to pass, while*
> *my glory passeth by, that I will put thee in a cleft of the*
> *rock, and will cover thee with my hand until I have passed*
> *by: and I will take away my hand, and thou shalt see my*
> *back; but my face shall not be seen. Exodus 33:21–23*

Why was it necessary for God to cover Moses, one of the most righteous men that we know in the Bible? Why should he be hidden or covered when God showed Himself to Him? Ask yourself this question. One day, every one of us is going to see the glory of the Lord. But you know the glory of the Lord could destroy us unless we were covered. The glory of the Lord would be like a million, million volts that could destroy us. He covered Moses.

> *And I have put my words in thy mouth, and have*
> *covered thee in the shadow of my hand, that I may plant*
> *the heavens, and lay the foundations of the earth, and*
> *say unto Zion, Thou art my people. Isaiah 51:16*

It is a most extraordinary statement to say that before God fulfills His purpose, He takes this one, puts His words in his mouth, and covers him with the shadow of His hand. God's hand is over him as a shadow.

And he hath made my mouth like a sharp sword; in
the shadow of his hand hath he hid me. Isaiah 49:2

He that dwelleth in the secret place of the Most High shall
abide under the shadow of the Almighty. Psalm 91:1

He will cover thee with his pinions, and under his wings shalt
thou take refuge: His truth is a shield and a buckler. Psalm 91:4

I will dwell in thy tabernacle for ever: I will take
refuge in the covert of thy wings. Psalm 61:4

Of Benjamin he said, The beloved of the Lord shall dwell
in safety by him; He covereth him all the day long and he
dwelleth between his shoulders. Deuteronomy 33:12

I will greatly rejoice in the Lord, my soul shall be joyful
in my God; for he hath clothed me with the garments of
salvation, he hath covered me with the robe of righteousness,
as a bridegroom decketh himself with a garland, and as
a bride adorneth herself with her jewels. Isaiah 61:10

O Lord, the strength of my salvation, Thou hast
covered my head in the day of battle. Psalm 140:7

Here we have a number of verses, representative of very many more, that deal with this matter of covering personally.

Tabernacle

Now we are going to look at one of the greatest symbolic things in the Old Testament—the tabernacle. Everything in the tabernacle was symbolic. It was a pattern of heavenly things.

And thou shalt make curtains of goats' hair for a tent over the tabernacle: eleven curtains shalt thou make them. Exodus 26:7

And the cubit on the one side, and the cubit on the other side, of that which remaineth in the length of the curtains of the tent, shall hang over the sides of the tabernacle on this side and on that side, to cover it. And thou shalt make a covering for the tent of rams' skins dyed red, and a covering of sealskins above. Exodus 26:13–14

First of all, you had the white, blue, scarlet and purple interwoven curtain. Above that, you had the rams' skins dyed red; and above that, you had the sealskins. Actually, we are not sure whether they were badger skins or sealskins. There were three coverings to the tabernacle and each one of them has meaning.

When the camp setteth forward, Aaron shall go in and his sons, and they shall take down the veil of the screen, and cover the ark of the testimony with it, and shall put thereon a covering of seal-skin and shall spread over it a cloth all of blue, and shall put in the staves thereof. And upon the table of showbread they

shall spread a cloth of blue, and put thereon the dishes, and the
spoons, and the bowls and the cups wherewith to pour out; and
the continual bread shall be there-on: and they shall spread
upon them a cloth of scarlet, and cover the same with a covering
of sealskin, and shall put in the staves thereof. Numbers 4:5–8

If you read all the way through down to verse 14 you find it is all
to do with covering. Every single bit of the tabernacle had to be
covered.

And they shall put upon it all the vessels thereof, wherewith
they minister about it, the firepans, the fleshhooks, and the
shovels, and the basins, all the vessels of the altar; and they
shall spread upon it a covering of sealskin, and put in the
staves thereof. And when Aaron and his sons have made
an end of covering the sanctuary, and all the furniture of
the sanctuary, as the camp is to set forward; after that,
the sons of Kohath shall come to bear it: but they shall not
touch the sanctuary, lest they die. Numbers 4:14–15

And the priests brought in the ark of the covenant of
the Lord unto its place, into the oracle of the house,
to the most holy place, even under the wings of the
cherubim. For the cherubim spread forth their wings
over the place of the ark, and the cherubim covered the
ark and the staves thereof above. II Chronicles 5:7–8

Why did the wings of the cherubim have to cover the ark?
They were so amazing that they covered, literally, the whole thing

from end to end, far beyond. You could just see the staves on either side coming out behind the curtain. The wings covered the whole. This is found in three different places in the Scripture.

The Glory of the Lord

Another circuit which I think is much more interesting is "The glory of the Lord". Here we come to what I find is a great mystery, but perhaps it is the key to this whole matter.

> *And Moses went up into the mount, and the cloud covered the mount. And the glory of the Lord abode upon mount Sinai, and the cloud covered it six days: and the seventh day he called unto Moses out of the midst of the cloud. And the appearance of the glory of the Lord was like devouring fire on the top of the mount in the eyes of the children of Israel. And Moses entered into the midst of the cloud, and went up into the mount: and Moses was in the mount forty days and forty nights. Exodus 24:15–18*

It is interesting that this connection between the glory of the Lord and something covering it comes again and again.

> *Then the cloud covered the tent of meeting, and the glory of the Lord filled the tabernacle. Exodus 40:34*

The cloud covered the tabernacle but the glory of the Lord filled the actual place.

> *And on the day that the tabernacle was reared up the cloud covered the tabernacle, even the tent of the testimony: and*

at even it was upon the tabernacle as it were the appearance
of fire, until morning. So it was alway: the cloud covered it,
and the appearance of fire by night. Numbers 9:15–16

And the Lord will create over the whole habitation of mount
Zion, and over her assemblies, a cloud and smoke by day,
and the shining of a flaming fire by night; for over all the
glory shall be spread a covering. And there shall be a pavilion
for a shade in the day-time from the heat, and for a refuge
and for a covert from storm and from rain. Isaiah 4:5–6

Cherubim

And under the firmament were their wings straight,
the one toward the other: every one had two which
covered on this side, and every one had two which
covered on that side, their bodies. Ezekiel 1:23

These cherubim had three pairs of wings–two pairs were used for covering themselves and one pair for flying. This is also found in Ezekiel 10 and a few other places in Scripture. What does it mean? We know that the cherubim are a composite symbol and they represent something. For instance, we find them in Revelation around the throne of God. If they are angels, they are the most hideous creatures you have ever seen; because whichever way you look, they have a different face. If you look from within they have one face; if you look from without they have another face; if you look from that side they have another face; and if you look from that side they have another face. They have wheels within wheels. They can go up; they can go down; they can go that way; they can go this way. They can go any angle from the wheels–wheels within wheels. Ezekiel speaks also of the whirring of the wheels. They have wings, but they only use one pair to fly. They have eyes all over, not only on their face and body but all over their wings; and the wheels are covered with eyes. The whole thing is symbolic of the glory of God, which was in them, and of the kind of creation that God wants.

> *In the year that king Uzziah died I saw the Lord sitting upon a throne, high and lifted up; and his train filled the temple. Above him stood the seraphim; each one had six wings; with twain he covered his face, and with twain he covered his feet, and with twain he did fly. Isaiah 6:1–2*

One pair of wings is for covering the eyes and the face. Now that is very strange because I don't know how any creature can cover its face so it can't see when it flies. One pair of wings is for covering the feet and one pair of wings is for flying. We begin to see there is something very mysterious in this whole subject about covering. Every detail of these visions has real meaning; and when the Scripture explicitly tells us about wings, for instance, how they are used or how they are not used, there is always a reason for it.

> *Thou wast the anointed cherub that covereth: and I set thee, so that thou wast upon the holy mountain of God; thou hast walked up and down in the midst of the stones of fire. Thou wast perfect in thy ways from the day that thou wast created, till unrighteousness was found in thee. By the abundance*

of thy traffic they filled the midst of thee with violence, and thou hast sinned: therefore have I cast thee as profane out of the mountain of God; and I have destroyed thee, O covering cherub from the midst of the stones of fire. Ezekiel 28:14–16

We know that the devil is the most intelligent being in the universe. We know that the devil, originally, had a position. He was called Lucifer, and in God's original economy, he had some position to do with worship and to do with covering. What does it all mean? In our reading through the Old Testament, we recognize that there is something far beyond us and something very important there.

Three Meanings of Covering

There are three Hebrew words that are used in the Old Testament in this matter of covering. One means "to conceal or to hide", which is the most common one used. The second means "to enclose or to hedge in". "Thou wast the anointed cherub that enclosed or hedged in." In Exodus 33, it says, "I will cover thee with my hand." That word is, "I will hedge thee in or I will enclose thee with my hand." The other reference in Isaiah, "I will cover thee with the shadow of my hand", is "I will conceal thee." There is a third word, not used so much, which means "to protect or to overlay", rather like a bird of prey. A larger bird overlays its young by bringing them into the soft downy part of its under belly. This is the word that is used when it says: "He shall cover him all the day long." He will overlay him like an eagle protects her young–concealed in that way. Obviously, this word "covering" means or speaks of protection, of safety, and of security.

In Christ

Now let's come to ground that perhaps we know a little better. Putting it in simple New Testament language, what it means to be covered is simply this: you are in Christ. This little phrase is used over two hundred times in the New Testament alone. To be covered means that you are in Christ.

> *Paul and Timothy, servants of Christ Jesus, to all the saints in Christ Jesus that are at Philippi, with the bishops and deacons. Philippians 1:1*

This little phrase "In Christ Jesus" occurs again and again in the Word. We know that when we believe, we believe into Christ. "For God so loved the world that He gave His only begotten Son that whosoever believeth on Him…"–that is the old version. Unfortunately, the very new, modern, colloquial versions have put "in"; but it does not really mean "in". It means our faith has carried us into Him. There is activity in it. We do not stand here and believe in Christ over there, but our faith carries us into Christ. Through our faith, God puts us in His own Son.

There are all kinds of phrases in the New Testament which sum up this matter of covering. Every time you read that you are in Christ, made to sit with Him, in Him in heavenly places, raised in Him, and all these other things, it is a question of being covered. You are in Him. That is where God has put you. If you have been saved by the grace of God, if you have been saved through the blood of Jesus Christ, if you have been born of the Spirit of God, you are in Christ. That is your position. God has put you there. That is your security. He is your stronghold; He is your fortress; He is the secret place of the Most High. That is the covert where God has put you—in Christ. Every single born again child of God has been placed in Christ by God. That is our position. Whether we are there in practice is another thing, but that is our position. Through faith in His Son, God has brought us into Him.

The Name

There are several phrases or matters that we associate with this. We speak of the name of the Lord.

> And whatsoever ye shall ask in my name, that will I do, that the Father may be glorified in the Son. John 14:13

What did the Lord Jesus mean? He did not mean that we just tack "In the name of Jesus Christ" on the end of our prayer like a little charm, and that works a miracle. Many Christians think that the name of Jesus is a charm, that all you have got to say is, "Jesus, Jesus", and something happens. Nothing happens unless the facts behind your use of that name are right. If the facts behind it are true and real, then you can take the name of Jesus on your lips and hell will quiver; but not otherwise. "In the name of Jesus"—what does it mean? It means that you are in Him.

I have four fingers and a thumb on one hand, and I have four fingers and a thumb on the other hand; and they are all in Lance Lambert. They are no one else's fingers and thumbs; they are in me. Now these fingers can say, "We can speak to you in the name of Lance Lambert." You have fingers and thumbs, but they cannot speak in my name; they speak in yours. When the Lord Jesus said, "Whatsoever ye shall ask the Father in my name that will I do", He meant, "When you are in me, you come to the Father in me." You simply say, "Father, we are not approaching You in our merits as if we are anything, as if we can get anything out of You"; we are approaching You in Thy Son; we are in Him. We have a right to His name." So "whatsoever you do, do all in the name of Jesus". Do everything as being in Christ. That is where you are. "Where two or three are gathered together in my name there am I in the midst of them" (Matthew 18:20). Here we are. We are gathered into the name because we are in Christ. All of us are in Christ; Christ is in all of us.

The Blood

Let us look at another phrase, "the blood of Jesus Christ". Some people have said to me after having terrible experiences of being carved up by the enemy, "I cannot understand it. I repeated again and again "the blood of Jesus, the blood of Jesus". But you cannot repeat "the blood of Jesus" and live in disobedience, as if by referring to the blood of Jesus you can take Satan in. If Satan knows he has got a foothold in your life through disobedience you cannot just say, "the blood of Jesus, the blood of Jesus". Satan just laughs. What you must do is get that matter put right under the blood of the Lamb. Then you can say, "In the blood of Jesus". When Satan comes and says, "What about that?"; you can say, "The blood of the Lamb, Father, the blood of the Lamb". There is peace in your conscience immediately; whereas, if the thing is still not settled and you go out, you have still got a bad conscience. You think, "I don't know; it doesn't work for me. They talk about being justified fully through Calvary's love, but it doesn't seem to work for me." Well, of course not! You cannot be unreasonable. This invisible world around us sees the reality of things.

But if we walk in the light, as he is in the light, we have fellowship one with another, and the blood of Jesus his Son cleanseth us from all sin. 1 John 1:7

Will you please note that there is an "if". Dear child of God, get this absolutely clear: if we do not walk in the light with God and we do not walk in the light with one another, then the blood of Jesus Christ, God's Son, does not go on cleansing. "If we confess our sins He is faithful to forgive us our sins"; but there must be confession. That word just simply means "to say the same thing"– to recognize what God calls it. If God says it is sin, I say it is sin. If God says it is disobedience, I say, "Lord, it is disobedience."

And be found in him, not having a righteousness of mine own, even that which is of the law, but that which is through faith in Christ, the righteousness which is from God by faith. Philippians 3:9

To be covered means that we are in Christ. We can speak in the name; we can act in the name. We are in Christ. The blood of Jesus Christ, God's Son, cleanses us continually from all sin. We are robed in the righteousness of the Lord Jesus Christ. It is as simple as that.

Abiding

There is another phrase that comes up in this matter of covering. In the last hours of His life, the Lord Jesus was at great pains to use one phrase over and over again: "Abide in me, abide in me." Again and again, He used it all the way through chapters 14, 15, and 16 of John. The last words to His own dear disciples were: "Abide in me." What did He mean? "Remain in me; that is your place of covering; that is where you are safe; that is where you are secure; that is where you are protected." "Abide in me and I in you."

> *For ye died, and your life is hid with*
> *Christ in God. Colossians 3:3*

That is covering. It is the armor of God. Have you found the Lord Jesus like that? Do you know Him as the "helmet of salvation"? Do you wear it? Are there times when your mind can be attacked because you do not have the helmet on? The head is the most vulnerable part in many ways. That is why we all need to find Christ as the helmet of salvation–covered!

Do you know Christ as truth–not just as the truth but as truth, as reality? "Having your loins girded with truth." In the modern versions it says, "Strapped or pulled in"; having the belt pulled in for strength with reality. If there is any unreality in our lives, we feel loose. Do you know Christ as reality?

"Breastplate of righteousness". Some of the modern versions say "integrity". That is over the heart–righteousness.

Do you have your feet shod with the preparation of the gospel of peace?

That is a hard word; but what it means is that you have your feet properly shod with good shoes peace. Do you know the peace of God? Do you know Christ as the peace of God? You cannot keep in the way of God without that peace. How do you know the will of God? "Let the peace of God arbitrate in your heart", or "Let the peace of God rule in your heart." You will know that you should go this way or that way by the peace of God. Your feet are shod with the gospel of peace, and the gospel is the way through which peace has come to you.

"Shield of faith". Do you know Christ as the shield of faith? This is the thing you can move about when the fiery darts come. Covering!

Uncovering

Perhaps we can understand this whole matter much more when we look at it from the negative side and what it means when we get uncovered. Many modern day believers refuse to believe that you can be weak or sick or even die. But 1 Corinthians 11:30 tells us that if we don't discern the body, that is the reality of the presence of Christ or what it is to be in Christ and Christ to be in us all, this can happen: weakness, sickness, death. Of course, people will say, "What kind of gospel is that?" But that is this whole matter of covering. Every one of us should take heed in this matter. People say, "How do you get uncovered?

I am getting frightened." Well, the best thing is to make sure that you are abiding. You do not have to fight to get under covering; you are there. All you have to do is to stay where God has put you; but when something has gone wrong, see that you put it right.

Something struck me the other day so forcibly. When we pray as we were taught to pray by the Lord Jesus, "Forgive us our trespasses as we forgive them that trespass against us" (Matthew 6:12), I wonder whether many of us understand what we are praying. We are asking God not to forgive us if we have not forgiven someone else. Do you realize that is uncovering? If I come before God and talk to God with unforgiveness in my heart, I am uncovered. There are forces that watch and say, "Ah ha, so he thinks he can get away with that. What are You going to do about it?" Remember the words of the Lord Jesus when He said: "Peter, Peter, Satan has obtained thee by request. I have prayed for thee that thy faith fail not" (Luke 22:31–32). What did He mean: "Satan hath obtained thee by request"? Go back a little earlier and you find that Peter said, "I will lay down my life for you, Lord." He did not know himself. In that moment, he was uncovered; and Satan went to God and said, "Did you hear that? Is it true? Let me have him." And God said, "You can have him, because there is something there that will come through, and what he will lose in the trial will be only what is not worth keeping." Jesus said: "I have prayed for you that your faith fail not." It did not. Even though he denied the Lord, his faith, deeper down than his denial, never failed. He came through.

Shall we pray?

Lord, Thou knowest every one of our hearts and the condition of each of our hearts. Lord, there is not one of us that wants to be uncovered. Therefore, we praise Thee and worship Thee for the safety and security which Thou has provided for us in the Lord Jesus Christ. Help every one of us, Lord, to walk in the light. Help every one of us, Lord, to be truly in Thee. Oh, may that truth be found in our inward parts. So Father, we commit this time to Thee deep, beyond us, mysterious but Thy Holy Spirit can give illumination to every one of our hearts. Grant, dear Lord, that that reverence for Thyself, that awe of Thyself, that loving, sensitive fear of the Lord which is the beginning of wisdom and the fountain of life to all who know it may be produced in us all. We ask it in the name of our Lord Jesus Christ. Amen.

2.
The Meaning of Covering

Psalm 91:1–4

He that dwelleth in the secret place of the Most High, shall abide under the shadow of the Almighty. I will say of the Lord, He is my refuge and my fortress; My God, in whom I trust. For he will deliver thee from the snare of the fowler, and from the deadly pestilence. He will cover thee with his pinions, and under his wings shalt thou take refuge: His truth is a shield and a buckler.

John 15:1–11

I am the true vine, and my Father is the husbandman. Every branch in me that beareth not fruit, he taketh it away: and every branch that beareth fruit, he cleanseth it, that it may bear more fruit. Already ye are clean because of the word which I have spoken unto you. Abide in me, and I in you. As the branch cannot bear fruit of itself, except it abide in the vine; so neither can ye, except ye abide in me. I am the vine, ye are branches: He that abideth in me, and I in him, the same beareth much fruit: for apart from me ye can do nothing. If a man abide not in me, he is cast forth as a branch, and is withered; and they gather them, and cast them into the fire, and they are burned. If ye abide in me, and my words abide in you, ask whatsoever ye will, and it shall be done unto you. Herein is my Father glorified, that ye bear much fruit; and so shall ye be my disciples. Even as the Father hath loved me, I also have loved you: abide ye in my love. If ye keep my commandments, ye shall abide in my love; even as I have kept my Father's commandments, and abide in his love. These things have I spoken unto you, that my joy may be in you, and that your joy may be made full.

Psalm 118:1–17

Oh give thanks unto the Lord; for he is good; For his lovingkindness endureth for ever. Let Israel now say, That his lovingkindness endureth for ever. Let the house of Aaron now say, That his lovingkindness endureth for ever. Let them now that fear the Lord say, That his lovingkindness endureth for ever. Out of my distress I called upon the Lord. The Lord answered me and set me in a large place. The Lord is on my side; I will not fear: What can man do unto me? The Lord is on my side among them that help me: Therefore shall I see my desire upon them that hate me. It is better to take refuge in the Lord Than to put confidence in man. It is better to take refuge in the Lord Than to put confidence in princes. All nations compassed me about; In the name of the Lord I will cut them off. They compassed me about like bees; they are quenched as the fire of *thorns: In the name of the Lord I will cut them off. Thou didst thrust sore at me that I might fall; But the Lord helped me. The Lord is my strength and song; And he is become my salvation. The voice of rejoicing and salvation is in the tents of the righteous: The right hand of the Lord doeth valiantly. The right hand of the Lord is exalted; The right hand of the Lord doeth valiantly. I shall not die, but live, And declare the works of the Lord.*

The matter of covering is a vitally important and necessary subject overlooked by the vast majority of Christians. It is because it is overlooked that there are so many casualties in the work of God, not only among young believers but, more especially, among those who are older in the Lord. Let no one think they are safe in this matter. Not even the Apostle Paul was safe. No one is safe unless they first see the danger that surrounds them and always hide themselves in the Lord Jesus Christ in a deliberate, defined act of faith, day by day. Whenever we feel a threatening from the enemy or from other things, such as circumstances or problems where we feel the enemy is in it, there should be a definite and deliberate act to hide ourselves in the Lord Jesus Christ. Therefore, for the walk of the believer, for the work of the believer, and for the warfare of the believer this matter is absolutely vital.

This matter is one of the most profound and mysterious subjects in the whole Word of God, for the simple reason that it is not just to do with time. Covering is not just to do with sin. It goes right back before sin was even found: "the anointed cherub that covereth"; "above the glory of God a covering". I cannot explain it. All I can tell you is that there is beyond us an infinity in this subject. Therefore, it behooves every one of us to be very humble in the presence of this matter and to recognize together that we are all learners.

Our Position: In Christ

What does covering mean? It is summed up in a New Testament phrase which is used over two hundred times: "In Christ". The child of God, the believer, the sinner saved by the grace of God, has been placed, by the sovereign power of God, in His Son. That is your position. If you are a child of God, if you are a believer, if you have been born of the Spirit, if you have been saved through the work of the Lord Jesus Christ at Calvary, then whether you know it or not, your position is in Christ. You are not just a subject of Christ or a person related to Christ, but your position is in Christ. That is where you are in the sight of God. You are in Him. He is not a child of God who is not in Christ. There is no such thing as a Christian who is not in Christ, for it is synonymous. It is impossible to be a child of God and not be in Christ. If you are a child of God, you are in Him.

We have been through a survey of the Old Testament from Genesis to Malachi. God seemed to be (to put it almost irreverently) harping on this matter again and again and again. On everything He did, He spoke of covering. We even find the cherubim with three pairs of wings, two of which they use for covering the face and feet and only one pair for flying. It is a most extraordinary message, but it all starts to become clear when you understand that every true believer is in Christ. That is your position. To be in Christ is to be covered. You are covered by what He is—His holiness, His purity, His spotlessness, His righteousness. All that He is before God covers you. You are in Him. If you are in Him, you cannot be seen out of Him. Why do so many Christians have consciences of evil? Why do so many Christians have hang-dog expressions? Why do so many Christians continually carry around this body of death, moaning all the time about it? It is because they have not seen that they are in Christ. Many Christians will say, "Oh yes of course, that is kindergarten." But they do not understand it. They think it is kindergarten but have never seen what it means.

What does it mean to be in Christ? It means we are in His holiness, covered by Him. When God looks, He sees Christ. When heaven looks, it sees Christ. We are in Him, hidden in Him. We are covered by what He is. Of course, this is what it means to be justified. It is so simple. It is quite fundamental, but do not think that anything fundamental is to be left behind. The foundation governs every single part of the building and carries all the weight of the building. This whole matter is tremendous!

Old Testament Pictures and Symbolism

Suddenly, we begin to find all the Old Testament pictures and symbolism start to mean something. They are summed up in this matter of being in Christ, covered in Him. Here are a few as they are found in the Scripture.

Stronghold: In Hebrew, "Metsudah" means stronghold. Christ is that to the believer. You can get right into Him; you are hidden in Him. A whole city can be hidden in that great Rock. He is fortress; He is stronghold; He is strong tower. "The righteous runneth into it and is safe" (Proverbs 18:10).

Refuge: He is refuge. He is the wings under which we have come to dwell. It speaks again and again of wings in the Old Testament. In Deuteronomy, it speaks a number of times of wings. Also, in many of the Psalms it speaks of wings. But it is all the same thing. We have come to dwell under His wings. His wings are like a protection that cover us–"In Christ".

Shield and Buckler: I don't really fully understand what a buckler is, but a shield is one kind of shield and a buckler is another kind of shield. Therefore, He is shield and shield; shield and buckler. He is the Rock in whom I take refuge.

House: He is the house. Now, that is something to think about. He is the house of God to which I come.

One thing have I asked of the Lord, that will I seek
after: That I may dwell in the house of the Lord
all the days of my life, To behold the beauty of the
Lord, And to inquire in his temple. Psalm 27:4

When you are in Christ, you will find He is the house of God. The house of God is not a building; the house of God is not an organization; the house of God is not an institution; the house of God is a Person: It is Christ. We come into Him as the temple of God. The Lord Jesus said: "Destroy this temple and in three days I will raise it up." They thought He spoke of that great building called the temple; but, in fact, He was speaking of His body. He spoke of something that was going to go into death, into burial and into resurrection. When it came out in resurrection, it was going to be the house of God, the temple of God forever—"In Him".

Sanctuary: The sanctuary is Christ. "When I came into the sanctuary then I understood." "I saw Thy ways O God in the sanctuary." In Christ you are hidden, covered in Him.

Tabernacle: The tabernacle had curtains all around. These curtains were of blue, scarlet, purple and white. They all spoke of Christ: of His redeeming work, of His heavenly nature, of His kingly nature, and of His absolute righteousness. Over that, there was another covering of goat skins; and over that, another covering of badger skins or seal skins (we are not quite sure what they were). There was covering after covering.

Every single thing speaks of some aspect of the Lord Jesus Christ. The tabernacle is the Lord

Jesus Christ: Some people say the tabernacle is the church, but this is not wholly true. The tabernacle speaks of the Lord Jesus Christ in all the aspects of His being, of His character, of His nature, of His work; and you and I have come into the tabernacle of God.

Pavilion: This is a word spoken of more as the palace. "He will hide me secretly in His pavilion" (Psalm 27:5). In another place it says: "He will hide me in His pavilion from the strife of tongues" (Psalm 31:20b). It is like a king taking someone into the palace and hiding him in the secret place of a strongly fortified and guarded palace. The Lord Jesus Christ is a pavilion into which you and I can come and be absolutely safe and feast with the King Himself.

Hiding Place: In many places in the Scripture, He is spoken of as a covert a covered place, something that is sort of secret. He is the secret place of the Most High.

All these Scriptures begin to take on meaning when you understand that they are all symbolic and all, in picture form, are setting forth the fact that the believer, the child of God, has been placed, by the sovereign power of God, in His Son. These are all different aspects of that work, but it is all finally coming to the same thing.

Offerings

However, there is something far more about this matter of being covered and it is found in Leviticus in the first seven chapters. Now, I know what some young believers may feel, because I can remember myself as a young believer just starting to read Leviticus and dying a million deaths. I could not think what all that business was about this offering and the law of this offering and that offering and the law of that offering. What did it have to do with us in the twentieth century? There was page after page, chapter after chapter, about details of each of these offerings; and it was, obviously, very important. It was years afterwards that I began to understand how vital and how practical all this business was about offerings.

There are five offerings in those chapters. There is the burnt offering, the meal offering, the peace offering, the sin offering, and the trespass offering. Christ is everyone of those offerings. He is the five-fold offering for us; He is the five-fold sacrifice for us; and it covers every single aspect of our relationship with God and with man. In other words, we are covered by the sacrifice of the Lord Jesus Christ. We are covered by the finished work of the Lord Jesus Christ, the offering up of Himself once, for all time.

Burnt Offering

This has not so much to do with sin. The burnt offering is all to do with service, with worship. Some people think that all you have got to do is consecrate yourself to God and fling yourself into the work of God. That is the surest way you will get uncovered. How does God receive anything? He burns it up. He takes the whole and consumes it. Is there anyone ready for this? But our Lord Jesus Christ has been offered up as the burnt offering. Listen to Him: "Lo, I come to do thy will. I delight to do thy will, O God; my ear hast thou digged" or opened (Psalm 40:6–8). God has got His ear. But my service must always fail. Why, if I had the zeal of the Apostle Paul and were to labor like he did; or if I had the revelation and understanding and passion of the Apostle John; still, I would need the Lord Jesus Christ as my burnt offering. I could not plead anything of myself. I could not say, "Oh God, see me; see what I have offered to you. See how devoted I am." The further I go, the deeper I go with God, the more I must plead the covering of the Lord Jesus Christ. He is my burnt offering. No service from me is acceptable apart from the Lord Jesus Christ.

Meal Offering

The meal offering speaks of humanity. God always mixes this in with the other offerings because it is meal and not meat. It speaks of the perfect humanity of the Lord Jesus Christ. Has anyone got perfect humanity? No! Oh, the kind of service we find so often in Christian circles mechanical, cold, hard, legal, according to regulation; it is not human. The one thing we see about the Lord Jesus Christ is humanity. The thing that shines through Him when God is most revealed in Him as God is His humanity.

How can I know that? The Lord Jesus was offered as that for me, and He is the only one who can bring that kind of humanity into me as the new man. If I try to bring my old nature in and polish it up and rehash it and present it to God as a new kind of humanity, it is an awful mess. However, God can produce something in me as I take the covering of the Lord Jesus Christ as the new man.

Peace Offering

The peace offering was the one offering that we all shared. If you took the offering to the temple in the old days, you went in, sat down, and ate it. First, the priests had their portion; then the Levites had their portion; and then it was handed back to you, and you and your family sat down in the temple courts and had a jolly good feast. It was called the peace offering, not only because it spoke of peace between you and God, but peace between you and your brother and sister. You could commune together, you could participate together, and you could share together.

Do you know Christ covering you as the peace offering? Our relationships are continually subjected to pressure. We have an enemy. All the time he breathes into our ear insinuations about one another. All the time he is trying to press things and relationships to the breaking point. Woe betide anyone who rests on this kind of line: "Well I like so-and-so; he and I will never get parted; she and I will never get parted because we are buddies; we are friends." You will find that when the devil gets to work, the dearest natural relationships will come to the breaking point. There is only one way through covering. The Lord Jesus Christ covers us because He was offered as our peace offering and it is Him that we share. It is Himself. Who is this offering that is offered up and given back to us to eat? It is Christ. As I offer up Christ, as I take back into my hands what God has offered for me, I share Him with you and you share Him with me. Our relationship is Christ; our unity is Christ. We do not agree to agree. We do not just try to make our opinions the same. We hold to the oneness of the Lord Jesus Christ. He is covering.

Sin Offering and Trespass Offering

If someone has committed sin, we all understand that the Lord Jesus Christ is the sin offering. But what about the trespass offering? In these democratic days when there are such cockeyed ideas all over the place, you find that many Christians get this attitude: "God won't hold me responsible for doing something that I didn't even know was sin." But that is just where you are wrong. You are just being subjective when you think that sin is only what you know to be sin. God help you. If you knew what sin really was, you would probably go into a mental home. It is in the mercy and grace of God that we do not understand the full capacity of sin and understand what we are capable of as human beings. We do not even understand what is inside us.

When a person sinned unwittingly, there was still an offering. When a person sins, they sin. The trespass offering speaks of God passing over sins because people did not know, but they were still sins. Just because they did not know it, it did not keep it from being sin. This is the thing that comes down again. Sometimes we come to a meeting and it is so heavy and so dark; it is unwitting sin. There is not a single soul in the company that could hold the Lord Jesus up as trespass offering. We have found again and again that in the brother's time on Sunday morning, when there has been a sense of heaviness and we have pleaded the Lord Jesus Christ as trespass offering and peace offering, immediately, the atmosphere has been broken. How do you explain that? Is it psychological or is it a matter of covering? Sin has been committed: people have talked unwisely; people have prayed unwisely; or someone has done something unwisely. Because we are all bound up together, we affect one another. The invisible forces around us know all about it. "Ha", they say, "we have got them"; and they come in like a flood. And what do people do? As soon as a heaviness comes they say, "Ohhh...so-and-so." We do blame flesh and blood. We really do blame flesh and blood. I know I am just as guilty, and probably more so, than others. We take hold of people and say, "It is so-and-so. If they pulled their socks up, it would be so different. If we had not sung that dreadful hymn at the beginning, it would all have been different." Then we blame so-and-so because so-and-so chose that hymn. It has nothing to do with flesh and blood at all, but this is where roots of bitterness begin. It has nothing to do with that at all. It has to do, perhaps, with something that no one knows about in a particular life; and that one does not even know himself that he has unwittingly sinned.

This five-fold covering covers something, not only to do with sin, but with service, worship, "presenting our bodies a living sacrifice, holy acceptable to God which is your spiritually intelligent worship or service", and comes right down to sin committed unwittingly. That is what it means to be in Christ. It means that God has given us a salvation so great, so tremendous, so infinite that not a single contingency, not a single emergency, not a single avenue of Satan needs to be opened up or needs to remain open because God has given us such a sacrifice, such a covering. We are covered.

I wish that there were those among us who could pray in this way, who, by the Spirit of God, knew when to take the Lord Jesus as burnt offering; who knew when to take the Lord Jesus as peace offering; who knew when to take Him as trespass and sin offering. You can only know that by anointing, but that is prayer. Some people are so insensitive and so dull that the only way they would know the devil was among them was if he appeared, physically, in front of their very eyes and gazed at them. Then they would say, "Oh, we must take the covering." How tragic that really is. If we were alive to God, if we were alive to the Spirit of God, there would be times when we would know there is something going on here and the only answer is the Lord Jesus. It is a question of covering or uncovering.

Three Ways of Being in Christ

There are three subjects that we find in the Word of God, in the New Testament, which sum up this whole matter of being in Christ in many ways.

Name of The Lord

If ye shall ask anything in my name, that will I do. John 14:14

And whatsoever ye do, in word or in deed, do all in the name of the Lord Jesus giving thanks to God the Father through him. Colossians 3:17

This is a very interesting word. It does not mean that when you pray you are to just tag on the end of your prayer "In the name of the Lord Jesus Christ". By all means say, "In the name of the Lord Jesus Christ" when you know what it means; but it is not a charm. It is not an "open Sesame". What does it mean? How do you do all things in the name of the Lord Jesus Christ? When you give a word, you do it in the name of the Lord Jesus Christ; but when you have a conversation, you also do it in the name of the Lord Jesus. Have you ever thought about that? That might shut some of us up. Let your talk be in the name of the Lord Jesus Christ.

Acts should be in the name of the Lord Jesus Christ. Do your shopping in the name of the Lord Jesus Christ. I am not being funny. Do your washing up in the name of the Lord Jesus Christ. Do your cleaning, or caring for the home, your work at the office, or at the college, your studies, or "Whatsoever ye do, do all in the name of the Lord Jesus Christ." Does it mean we become sanctimonious and say to the person from whom we buy our soap, or whatever, "I am buying it in the name of the Lord Jesus Christ"? Of course not! You understand that as well as I do. But what does it mean? The Scripture is not foolish. It says, "Do all whether in word or deed in the name of the Lord Jesus." It means simply this: you are in Him; do everything from a covered position. Never do the most innocuous job outside of covering, whatever it is. Remember there are invisible rays from another world that would hit you and bring you down once you are uncovered.

"Do all in the name of the Lord Jesus." What does it mean? All the members of my body are in Lance Lambert; so everything they do, word or action, is in the name of Lance Lambert. When I eat, it is Lance Lambert. When I speak, it is Lance Lambert.

When I gesticulate, it is Lance Lambert. When I walk, it is Lance Lambert. Everything I do or say is in the name of Lance Lambert. "Do all in the name of the Lord Jesus." You are in Him. You cannot say, "There is a spiritual side to my life and there is a secular side to my life. When I go to a meeting, of course, I am more godly there. Then there is my other side when I get home, put my slippers on, and roll down my hair." There is no such thing as that. You are either in Christ or out of Him. You cannot do anything outside of Him if God has put you in Him. God says, "Remember that; do everything as being in Him." Let me remind you of the Old Testament:

> The name of the Lord is a strong tower; The righteous runneth into it, and is safe. Proverbs 18:10

That is where we are meant to be: in the strong tower which is the Lord Jesus Christ.

The Blood of Christ

> But if we walk in the light, as he is in the light, we have fellowship one with another, and the blood of Jesus his Son cleanseth us from all sin. 1 John 1:7

The blood of Christ speaks of peace. It speaks of being nigh to God. It speaks of access, immediate, instantaneous access to God. It speaks of victory. "They overcame him (the devil) through the blood of the Lamb." It speaks of life. Oh, to know life. The life is in the blood. We know eternal life as, continually, we know what it is to be under the covering of the blood. However, some people think they can just use the phrase "the blood of the Lamb" and that is enough; it works a miracle. Not so! The Scripture has an "if". "If we walk in the light as God is in the light ..." It is not as we see the light, but "if we walk in the light as God is in the light (that is objective) we have fellowship one with another and the blood of Jesus Christ, God's Son cleanses us from all sin."

> *And the blood shall be to you for a token upon the houses*
> *where ye are: and when I see the blood, I will pass over*
> *you, and there shall no plague be upon you to destroy*
> *you, when I smite the land of Egypt. Exodus 12:13*

God sees the blood of His Son upon everyone who is saved by His grace. You do not see it, but God sees it. And when God sees it, He passes over; you are covered. It is possible to come out from under that covering by not walking in the light, but that is another matter. When we are walking in the light, we remain under covering. The blood goes on covering us; it goes on cleansing us. What a victory it was! When the first-born of Egypt was smitten that night and died, it spelt the end for Egyptian power. The power of Pharaoh and the power of Egypt was broken that night by the blood of the Lamb. Any Hebrew who did not have the blood on his house was visited by the angel of death, and any Egyptian that had the blood upon his house was passed over. Think about that!

The Righteousness of Christ

Him who knew no sin he made to be sin on our
behalf; that we might become the righteousness
of God in him. II Corinthians 5:21

In him" We are prone to miss that. "We might become the righteousness of God in him." God has removed my sin by the blood of the Lamb, by the work of the Lamb; but He has placed me in Him where I am made righteous, declared righteous, justified, acquitted and covered.

I will greatly rejoice in the Lord, my soul shall be joyful in my
God; for he hath clothed me with the garments of salvation, he
hath covered me with the robe of righteousness ... Isaiah 61:10

Do you know anything about the garment of salvation? Do you know how to use the garment of salvation? Some people come in on Sunday morning and it is quite clear they have on the spotted garment of their own doings. You can almost see it looking out of their eyes. "Oh, it is no good me praising the Lord." And the devil says, "Quite right! You are hopeless. Look at that; look at that; look at that." "Oh God, here I am at your table. Do forgive me. I can hardly lift my eyes up." But if you are not living in habitual sin, there is a garment of salvation. "What have you done coming into the wedding feast without your garment on?" The Lord could be angry and say, "Out with that person. How dare they come into My presence and think that something of their own doing is going to satisfy Me. Have I not provided the garment of salvation?

They could have come in the garment of salvation and I would have said, "You are all fair, My love. There is no spot in you." Some people get a terrible shock when the Lord says to them, "I don't find anything wrong in you.

Do you remember when Balaam had to prophesy about the children of Israel? They were, in one sense, the most rebellious, godless lot you ever saw. They were murmuring and complaining, chattering to one another about how they would like to go back to Egypt, why God had brought them out into the desert, and all the rest of it. Balaam said, "The Lord says, 'I see no iniquity in Jacob.'" Have you ever heard of such a thing? Why did God see no iniquity in Jacob? It was because of the Passover Lamb. Their sin was covered. "Covered all my unrighteousness".

Do you know how to use the garment of salvation? More Christians suffer from depression and, in the end, oppression from the enemy because they do not know how to use the robe of righteousness, the garment of salvation. Having been saved by the grace of God, they slip off the garment of salvation and start to walk before God as if they were something. But it is the garment of salvation. Covered.

Hid with Christ in God

For ye died, and your life is hid with
Christ in God. Colossians 3:3

When something is hidden, you cannot find it; it is lost to view. Where is your life? Your life is lost in God. "Hid with Christ in God." Think of the infinity of what God is. God has hid your life with Christ in Himself. When the devil comes and says, "Where is Lance Lambert? I am going to get him", God says, "I am sorry, you cannot find him. He is hid with Christ in Me."

That is just where Peter failed. Peter came out from the covering and said to the Lord, "Die? You die? Never!" He contradicted the will of God. Of course, it was the natural thing to do. Wouldn't you have done it? If the Lord Jesus said, "I am going to die today", wouldn't you have said, "Never, over my dead body"? How did he get out of covering? Most people think he was presumptuous. No, he wasn't presumptuous. He was quite spontaneous. He contradicted the will of God. Some people say ignorance is bliss, but others say ignorance is dangerous. He did not know what he was doing; therefore, he spoke inadvisably and Satan heard it. Satan went before God and said, "Peter, Peter, let me have him." God was unable to say, "He is hid with My Son in Me." He said, "All right, he has come out from under covering. You have him." The Lord Jesus said to Peter: "Simon, Simon, Satan hath obtained thee by request but I prayed for thee that Thy faith fail not" (Luke 22:31–32 RV). This teaches us one of the biggest lessons in how we can get uncovered.

"Hid with Christ in God." When something is hid it cannot be found except in Him. If I want to find you and you are in Christ, I have to find Christ. If I am going to find you, I find you in Christ. I meet Christ. Isn't it wonderful when the enemy is after you, he comes up against Christ? The pillar of cloud and the pillar of fire came between the enemy and the people of God and confused the enemy so that he could not see. That is covering. Perhaps you begin to understand why this matter is so vital. Do you see the whole point of staying where God has put you?

Abiding in Christ

I am the vine, ye are the branches: He that abideth
in me, and I in him, the same beareth much fruit:
for apart from me ye can do nothing. John 15:5

"Abide in me and I in you." Does it mean that, somehow, I have to fight through to getting into Christ? No! You abide in Him. The word "abide" means "remain", "stay", "continue", or "dwell". Continue where God has put you. Stay where God has put you. Where has God put you? He has put you in Christ. Don't get out; stay there. If you have gotten out, get back. Get back immediately, whatever the cost. While you are uncovered, you are in terrible spiritual danger. Anything can get you while you are uncovered, and that is why the Lord Jesus intercedes.

Many people ask me why the Lord Jesus ever lives to intercede at the right hand of God. Surely God knows what He is going to do anyway. Surely God can do what He is going to do anyway. Of course God knows what He is going to do and can do what He is going to do anyway. That is not the point. The Lord Jesus intercedes for those who get out from under covering. "I have prayed for you, Simon", and in that one statement, we have the foreshadowing of the intercession of the Lord Jesus at the right hand of God. Oh, I thank God for the prayers of the Lord Jesus for myself. No wonder the old Puritans used to write whole books on intercession. You never hear of such things today. If you get a book at all, it is about our intercession. But the old Puritans used to write books on the intercessory ministry of the Lord Jesus Christ at the right hand of God, because they, seeing something of the sovereignty of God, know that the only thing that would ever get them, finally, before His face would be the intercession of the Lord Jesus Christ. Left to ourselves, we are so dumb, so stupid, so insensitive, we would be out from covering straightaway.

The Whole Armor of God

"Abide in me and I in you." We are covered by that, and that is what it means to put on the whole armor of God. You know those words so well in Ephesians 6:10–18; but have you ever noticed the little commentary, in one sense, on it in Romans?

> *The night is far spent, and the day is at hand: let us therefore cast off the works of darkness, and let us put on the armor of light. Let us walk becomingly, as in the day; not in revelling and drunkenness, not in chambering and wantonness, not in strife and jealousy. But put ye on the Lord Jesus Christ, and make not provision for the flesh, to fulfil the lusts thereof.* Romans 13:12–14

It is the lusts of our flesh; or, to put it in another way, the natural desires of the flesh, which may be legitimate or illegitimate, which are the things that so often entice us and bring us out. "Put on the armor of light." Put on the Lord Jesus Christ and make no provision for the flesh so that it does not have a chance. It is not only the enemy from without, but it is the enemy from within.

Notice in Ephesians 6 that it says, "Put on the armor of God." It says nothing of the kind! It says, "Put on the whole armor of

God." It is a sobering fact that you can put on ninety per cent of the armor and leave off one part and the enemy will get you. There is no point in my dressing myself up like a human tank and leaving my helmet off. I am a sure target for the enemy to blast my head off. There is no point in my taking a shield and not having the breastplate of righteousness, for while I am shielding off something there, something hits me, and I am done for. What is the point of being absolutely clad in armor and not having the shoes on? Do you realize how vulnerable feet are? If you were in an army with all those people clad in armor and you let one of them tread on your toes, you wouldn't even need the enemy. Your feet are vulnerable unless they are clad. It is so interesting that the Scripture speaks of putting on the whole armor and this is where we all fail. Some of us have the helmet on but we have not got the shield of faith on. Some of us have the shield of faith on, but we have not got the breastplate on or we have not got our loins girt strongly with truth and reality.

"Put on the whole armor of God that we may, thus covered, be enabled to stand and to withstand and having done all to stand." Isn't this just another way of saying "abide"? Isn't it interesting that it says, "Having done all to stand"; and not, "Having done all you march forward a thousand miles"? This battle is not a question of going forward; this battle is won by abiding. It is a victory already won which has got to be ratified. When we see that, it makes a great change. This is not a kind of victory where we have got to go forward. It is a victory where we stand still in Him. We abide in Him. We are covered; and as we remain covered, so it is won. It is ratified; it is expressed; it is manifested; it is registered.

Security

We see that there is, in Christ, absolute safety, absolute security, absolute protection. The youngest child of God has no need to fear. There is a hymn we sing, A Debtor to Mercy Alone, in which the last verse has given some a bit of a problem.

Yes, I to the end shall endure, as sure as the earnest is given. More happy but not more secure, the glorified spirits in heaven.

In some of our hymn books, they changed that last line because so few people understood what it meant. It means this: all those people in glory are not more secure than you and I down here. If you let that sink into you, it will change your whole attitude to Satan, to the enemy and to darkness. You think, "They must be more secure." No! They are, of course, beyond the reach of the enemy, but they are not more secure. You are beyond the reach of the enemy if your life is hid with Christ in God. If you could only see that by remaining under covering, you are as secure as they. How can the enemy get hold of you if you are in Christ? He has got to deal with Christ; and therefore, if God says, "Yes, you can come through Christ", He is going to do something in you that is absolutely marvelous. It can be heaven. It is not in the same category at all as destruction, disintegration, and deterioration.

"More happy ... " Oh yes, they are more happy. I think of some we know up there. I say, "Up there"; they are probably all around, because heaven is only another dimension. I think of Auntie Anna. She is more happy, but she is not more secure; and I expect if she can hear me, she would say "Amen". I think of others. They are more happy, but not more secure. They are in Christ. And where are you? You are in Christ! Are they more in Christ than you? No! Then what is the difference? They are those who are the dead in Christ and we are, as it says in the old prayer book, "the quick in Christ". There is no difference. This is why the devil would blind you to it and try to make you think that you are second class citizens of heaven and those up there are first class. Not so! The creed says this: "I believe in the communion of saints." This does not mean the communion of living saints on earth. It means "the absolute sharing of the whole". It is one church, part in the presence of the Lord, the rest on earth. "I believe in the communion of saints, the one holy church."

There is something very wonderful about this whole thing. You are not more happy than they; I am not; that is something to come. But you are not less secure. You are only less secure in so far as you come out from under covering. Let the enemy entice you out, let him get you to say something ill-advised, let him get you to do something in darkness, let him get you to collide with someone and not put it right, let him get you to contradict the will of God, and he has got you out. If you do not know how to get back immediately, you are in for trouble. You and I have got to learn how to get back under covering. Those who have responsibility in the work of God, and, in the end, that shall be everyone of us, must learn how to take Christ as our five-fold offering and plead Him for the whole for those who do not know what they are doing.

Do you remember that when Job's friends did some very stupid things, they angered the Lord because they got uncovered? The Lord said to Job, "Stand back, Job. I will wipe them out." They came to Job and the Lord said to them, "You go and ask Job to pray for you and if Job prays for you, I will hear." So much for democracy in that sense. They had done something quite wrong.

"Oh," you say, "that is quite unjust." No, it isn't. They had not suffered like Job. They should never have spoken in the way they did, using all those wonderful highfalutin phrases about this and this and this. Some of the things those friends said are really rather wonderful, but it would have been much better if they had shut up and written a book of their own. It would have been the Book of Bildad and we would have those wonderful thoughts of Bildad that had nothing to do with Job at all. But they tried to apply them to Job's situation and say, "Job, you are a sinner; Job, you have done this; this is the reason for it all." It was Job who had to pray, "Oh God, forgive them," and God said, "I will."

The children of Israel murmured against the Lord and the Lord said to Moses: "Stand back, I will destroy the lot of them. Furthermore, I will make of you a nation stronger and greater than they." That should have produced something out of Moses. If he could only have been enticed, he would have come out and said: "Oh, now that is something. I have suffered this lot for forty years. I think it might be better if they were like me, my type of nature and character." But Moses would not come out from under covering. He said: "Lord, You just remember who You are. Just You think what the nations will say when they have heard that You brought them up out of Egypt." The Lord smiled and thought: "Moses is just like Me. He has got the same kind of nature as I have. Of course, I can't destroy them. Right, Moses; you pray for them and I will forgive them." And Moses prayed. Oh, for a ministry that can take hold of Christ, the five-fold aspect of His offering, and plead it for all. I have seen believers kept in spiritual life by the secret prayer of people, when they should have been struck down. That is the question of covering. "The fear of the Lord is the beginning of wisdom."

The Lord Jesus taught us to pray a pattern prayer: "Lead us not into trial" (Matthew 5:13). The New English Bible puts it: "Don't put us to strong test but deliver us from the evil one." Every time you pray, say, "Father, don't put us to the test, but deliver us from the evil one." What it really means is this: don't let us get uncovered. When we are under fire or under temptation, don't let us come out. "Oh Father, preserve us from it that the enemy does not get hold of us because we have been uncovered."

Shall we pray?

Father, we do pray that Thou will, in some real way, write this tremendous subject on our hearts. Some of us understand just a little about it. For others of us, it is altogether new. Lord, we don't want the wrong kind of fear and self-consciousness to come upon us so that, spiritually, we are inhibited. Oh Lord, we do need to know what it is to be in Thy Son in practice, to know the provision which is ours, the fulness which is ours, the blessings which are ours, all that is ours in Him—protection, security, safety. Father, hear us. We commit ourselves to Thee. Write this lesson indelibly upon our heart. May it be for all of us, perhaps, the beginning of an understanding of this matter that will stand us in good stead in the days to come. Our Father, who art in heaven, Hallowed be thy name. Thy kingdom come. Thy will be done, as in heaven, so on earth. Give us this day our daily bread. And forgive us our debts, as we also have forgiven our debtors. And bring us not into temptation, but deliver us from the evil one. Amen.

3.
The Danger of Getting Uncovered

Read Psalm 91:1–16; 118:1–17

Psalm 118:18–29

The Lord hath chastened me sore; But he that not given me over unto death. Open to me the gates of righteousness: I will enter into them, I will give thanks unto the Lord; This is the gate of the Lord; The righteous shall enter into it. I will give thanks unto thee; for thou hast answered me, And art become my salvation. The stone which the builders rejected Is become the head of the corner. This is the Lord's doing; It is marvellous in our eyes. This is the day which the Lord hath made; We will rejoice and be glad in it. Save now, we beseech thee, O Lord: O Lord, we beseech thee, send now prosperity. Blessed be he that cometh in the name of the Lord: We have blessed you out of the house of the Lord. The Lord is God, and he hath given us light: Bind the sacrifice with cords, even unto the horns of the altar. Thou art my God, and I will

*give thanks unto thee: Thou art
my God, I will exalt thee. Oh
give thanks unto the Lord; for he*   *is good; For his lovingkindness
endureth for ever.*

Shall we pray?

*Dear Lord, we do once more tell Thee we are utterly dependent upon
Thee both for speaking and hearing alike. Take, dear Lord, this time
and make it live to us we pray. Hide the poor lips and grant, we pray,
our beloved Lord, that we shall hear what Thy Spirit has to say to us.
We ask it in the name of our Lord Jesus. Amen.*

We want to speak about the danger of getting uncovered.
Of necessity, it is going to be a little more negative and, I dare say,
to some a little frightening. However, we will trust that the Lord
will make something much more positive over it all and help us to
keep our eyes clearly on Him. If the believer is in Christ, what is
the danger of getting uncovered? Satan has an overall objective,
one supreme aim upon which he bases his whole strategy and
plan; and it is to get the child of God uncovered. It is precisely
the same with the church. We speak of the recovery of the church.
It is the enemy's objective, concerning the whole church, to get it
uncovered and thus to destroy it. It is the supreme aim of Satan
to get the work of God, in its many aspects, uncovered. He has
got to draw us out of Christ. He has got to entice us away from
our position in Him so that we are no longer abiding in Him,
no longer remaining where God has placed us. Positionally,

we are there; but practically, we are out. The enemy's whole plan is to entice us. He cannot do it by just saying, "Look here, get out." Every child of God, even the youngest believer, would recognize that as Satan. If something shouted at you or if something even whispered at you, "Get out of Christ, get out of Christ; don't abide in Him; it is not safe for you; it is not good for you to abide in Him", we would say, "That is the enemy; I will resist that." But Satan is the most intelligent being in the universe and his intelligence has been passed on to the whole hierarchy of evil. He knows exactly what he is up against. He is not going to make a frontal attack like that. By wile, by guile, by deceit, as an angel of light or a minister of righteousness with all the appearance of good, he is going to entice us so that, slowly but surely, he can draw us out from our position and get us uncovered.

The devil is very much like a chameleon. He colors himself to his surroundings and so he watches us. He finds out our weaknesses–our temperamental weaknesses, weaknesses that come from our background, weaknesses that come from our circumstances–and he colors himself so perfectly to our circumstances, to our weaknesses, to our failings, that we have great difficulty, sometimes, distinguishing that it is the work of Satan at all. If Satan cannot get us to be careless about putting on the whole armor of God then he will seek to get us careless about one vital piece. There are some believers who do not know how to put on the whole armor of God and so to be able to stand. When he finds a believer who does know how to hide in the Lord, does know how to abide in the Lord, then he turns his attention to getting them to leave one particular and vital piece of the armor out, whatever that might be, so that, in one way or the other, his supreme aim can be reached. That aim is to get us out from under covering.

Absolute Safety in Christ

Satan knows better than any believer that the child of God has absolute safety in Christ. He knows that there is nothing he can do until the child of God is uncovered. Let that sink into you, because it is the positive side of it. There is absolute safety for every child of God. While we abide in Christ, Satan cannot reach us. He has to meet with Christ first. "Our life is hid with Christ in God." Before Satan can discover us, before Satan can reach us, before he can touch us, he has got to come to God and Christ. When we are abiding in Him, the first person he meets is Christ. He meets the righteousness of Christ, the power of Christ, the authority of Christ, the mercy of Christ, the grace of Christ, the work of Christ. He meets it all before he can get at the believer. When we are abiding in Christ, there is absolute security. Let your hearts be lifted up as it says in the Scripture:

Confirm the feeble knees and lift up the
hands that droop. Hebrews 12:12

Do not let the enemy, by his propaganda, get you to believe that it is almost a lost cause; that we are all so stupid, all so dimwitted that we are bound to get uncovered; and that we are bound to have a lot of trouble from Satan. Trouble? Yes; but it is the trouble that comes to the Lord Jesus first. In other words, there is a wonderful safety for the child of God while he abides in Christ, while he remains hid with Christ in God, while he has the whole armour upon him. Satan knows that there is absolutely nothing he can do until he has got us out of that position. Therefore, with all his intelligence, with all his deceit, with all his guile, he will do every single thing to get us out; nor will he give up. If he has not got you out in a year, he will go on for a second year, a third year, a fourth year, ten years, twenty years, thirty years. Right at the very end, he will try to get you out; he will not leave. His whole aim and objective is to get you uncovered and get you out. You may be young in the Lord; the enemy is out for you, to try and get you out. You may be old in the Lord; the enemy is out after you, to get you from under covering.

Victory Through Christ

It is much more than just a question of negatively being safe in Christ. Let your hearts be lifted once more on this whole matter. You are safe in Christ; no harm can come to you; the enemy cannot touch you; he cannot reach you while you are in God's Son. Not only that, but Satan knows very well that while we are in Christ, we must win. He knows that he can do nothing about it. It is a battle already fought and won; and that is why we have the most wonderful Scriptures that Satan cannot bear.

> But thanks be unto God, who always leadeth us in triumph
> in Christ, and maketh manifest through us the savor of
> his knowledge in every place. II Corinthians 2:14

If the Apostle Paul had only said, "sometimes leads us in triumph in Christ", it would still have been marvelous in our eyes. But he said: "always leads us in triumph in Christ". Another version puts it that the believer has been put in "the train of Christ's triumph". It is Christ who is the victor. It is Christ who has won, and the believer is in the train.

> *But thanks be to God, who giveth us the victory through our Lord Jesus Christ. Wherefore, my beloved brethren, be ye stedfast, unmovable, always abounding in the work of the Lord, forasmuch as ye know that your labor is not vain in the Lord. 1 Corinthians 15:57–58*

Satan knows that through Christ victory is given to us. It is given to us. It is an already obtained victory. It is given to us. You will notice this particular victory he is talking about is all to do with people who are dead. Can they do anything about raising themselves from the dead? Of course not! But the Scripture says: "Thanks be unto God who giveth us the victory through our Lord Jesus Christ."

The whole lot will rise in Christ. That is the kind of victory that is ours and Satan cannot do a single thing about it. Every time we put a dear believer's body into the ground, we signal the end of Satan's reign, the end of his power. So great is this victory of our Lord Jesus Christ that not even the bodies of the saints are going to be left. They are going to be raised incorruptible. The redemption of our Lord Jesus Christ is so great that it covers the body. That is the victory which is ours, obtained for us through Calvary.

If I go into the grave one day, and the Lord tarries for another twenty or thirty years, what will become of my body? There won't be much left of it after thirty years, and I will not be able to do anything about it. I may be in the presence of the Lord, beholding the face of the Lamb, but when the trumpet of God sounds, that old body of mine, that corruptible thing which has gone back to dust, gone back to earth, will be brought back together and reconstituted into a redemption body like His. What a victory! Now if the victory means that, what about the kitchen sink? What about the children? What about the office? Satan knows that in Christ we have the victory.

It is not that we are negatively safe; it is that we are positively victorious. Victory does not just mean that we have one of those seraphic, theatrical smiles that we pin up from ear to ear. Some people think victory is that kind of thing, but it is not. When the Psalmist said, "I shall yet praise God who is the help of my countenance" (Psalm 42:11), that was victory. He could not praise the Lord at that point, but he said I will do so. I will get through this. Satan wrung his hands when he heard the Psalmist say that, and wrung them even more when he wrote it down. "How could some believer say such a thing when I have made him so miserable that his chin is on the ground? There he sits down and says, "I shall yet praise God. How is he going to praise God? I will make it worse for him." The Psalmist is saying, "It is not just going to be that things are going to turn or that my circumstances are going to turn. It is going to be that, suddenly, the Lord is going to bring me out of it to a place where I can praise. Victory is mine." "Thanks be unto God who giveth us the victory through our Lord Jesus Christ."

The only way you will get victory is through our Lord Jesus Christ. If you and I are put in the earth one day, the way our bodies will be raised is through our Lord Jesus Christ. Therefore, if God can work a miracle like that and all the saints from the whole age are going to be raised incorruptible, be stedfast and unmovable, then don't let the kitchen sink move you out of Christ. Stay in Him. You are unassailable when you are in Him. Satan cannot touch you while you are in Christ. In that office which is so difficult, with that brother who you find so terribly difficult, or that sister who you can hardly get on with, don't get moved away. Don't let the enemy push you out of your place in Christ. Victory, then, is not just some bubbly thing; it is something which is deep and intensely practical.

Nay, in all these things we are more than conquerors through him that loved us. Romans 8:37

If only he had said: "By being delivered from all these things we are more than conquerors." That is how many people read this, but it does not say that. It says: "In all these things we are more than conquerors through Him that loved us." In some of our new versions, it changes the preposition to "in"; but it does not matter whether it is "through" or "in"; it means the same thing. In nakedness, in peril, in all these things, we are more than conquerors through Him that loved us. When we are in Christ, we are more than conquerors. Out of Christ, we are abject failures, absolutely defeated. We may have all the knowledge of the Bible in the world; we may have a past testimony of God's goodness and grace; but it stands us in no good stead if we have moved out of Christ, for then we are a contradiction in terms. Here we are the child of God–abject defeat. Here we are children of God–absolutely bound. Here we are children of God, and we do not know, or are not experiencing, what it is to be "being saved".

... and raised us up with him, and made us to sit with him
in the heavenly places, in Christ Jesus. Ephesians 2:6

No wonder the apostle says, "Don't forget; whatever else you do forget, don't forget to put on the whole armor of God that you may be able to stand in the evil day and having done all to stand." The apostle has seen something. He has seen that the weakest believer in Christ is unassailable, and the strongest believer outside of Christ is defeated. He has seen that the person with the most superficial knowledge of the Lamb, who yet remains in Christ, will be absolutely victorious; and the person who could write tomes on the Bible, who moves out of Christ, will be absolutely paralyzed. Victory! Satan knows that we are not only negatively safe and secure in Christ, he knows that in Him we are victorious. Therefore, Satan must get us to uncover ourselves. If he is to paralyze the work of God, if he is to frustrate the work of God, if he is to destroy the effectiveness of God's working, he has got to get the believers to uncover themselves. While they are in Christ, he can do nothing.

Warnings about Getting Uncovered

We are, of course, warned many times about this danger. We have already pointed out in the last two studies the many,

many warnings through the Word. I want to add a few more which are very, very solemn indeed.

Satan Roams as A Roaring Lion

Be sober, be watchful: your adversary the devil, as a roaring lion, walketh about, seeking whom he may devour. 1 Peter 5:8

What solemn words! Most of us do not think the devil would ever get us, let alone devour us; but the Apostle Peter, writing to elders as well as to the church, says: "Be sober"–this is a serious business. "Be watchful"–don't go to sleep, don't turn off; and if you are on one of those trips all around the world just at present in your mind, come back. "For your adversary the devil, as a roaring lion..." Wouldn't you think a believer could hear a roaring lion? I am told if you go to the Safari Park at feeding time, you can hear them roar. With all the windows wound up and the doors tightly closed and going through at a gentle 15 mph, you can hear clearly the roar of the lions. But some believers are so unwatchful, they never hear the roar of Satan. He is hungry! He is walking about, seeking whom he can devour.

How can he devour anyone in Christ? He must first devour Christ. How can he devour anyone whose life is hid with Christ in God? He must first devour God. Can Satan devour God? The only way he can get at your life is to devour God, and thus devour Christ and you. But he cannot do it. So he walks about to see who is out of covering, who has got out of Christ, or who is not abiding; and in that moment, he has got his meal. Oh, many of us have been meals, at times, for Satan; and what a meal! When Satan gets us, he really has a meal.

We shall come later to the wonderful ministry of our Lord Jesus Christ, without which none of us would ever come through. Thank God for that ministry. However, just at the moment, we have this rather more sobering thing.

> *And the great dragon was cast down, the old serpent, he that is called the Devil and Satan, the deceiver of the whole world; he was cast down to the earth, and his angels were cast down with him. And I heard a great voice in heaven, saying, Now is come the salvation, and the power, and the kingdom of our God, and the authority of his Christ: for the accuser of our brethren is cast down, who accuseth them before our God day and night. And they overcame him because of the blood of the Lamb, and because of the word of their testimony; and they loved not their life even unto death. Therefore rejoice, O heavens, and ye that dwell in them. Woe for the earth and for the sea: because the devil is gone down unto you, having great wrath, knowing that he hath but a short time. Revelation 12:9–12*

There is only one safe place for us to be and that is in the heavenlies, seated with Christ in heavenly places. "Then we will overcome by the blood of the Lamb, by the word of our testimony because we love not our lives even unto death." Woe to us if we come down to the earth, descend to the flesh and take again the old man as the basis. Satan has come down to that realm and he will try to get everyone who is found on it.

Physical Destruction of the Flesh

For he that eateth and drinketh, eateth and drinketh
judgment unto himself, if he discern not the body.
For this cause many among you are weak and sickly,
and not a few sleep. 1 Corinthians 11:29–30

This is not just to do with the actual Lord's table and the taking of bread and wine. This is to do with what that bread and wine symbolize, represent, or express. It says that it is possible, because we do not discern the body of our Lord Jesus Christ, to so get ourselves uncovered that we become weak, that is paralyzed, ineffective, bound; or sickly, which could mean that the plagues we are promised will not come to us, will come to us, either physically or spiritually; or sleep, which you all well know is not some poetic little word about just falling asleep spiritually, but means to physically die. So serious is this matter of uncovering that it is possible, not to lose one's salvation, but to lose one's physical life.

"If any man see his brother sinning a sin not unto death, (that is physical death, not spiritual death) he shall ask, and God will give him life for them that sin not unto death. There is a sin unto death: not concerning this do I say that he should make request." 1 John 5:16

Oh, how well some of us knew that Scripture when we prayed for a certain person and prayed and prayed and prayed. We did not understand that Scripture in those days. We prayed for that person's healing and every time we prayed, at the very moment we prayed "in the name of the Lord", they had a far worse attack.

Finally, one dear old brother phoned me up and said, "I cannot understand it; I have been the whole morning in prayer for so-and-so, but the Lord has said to me that I was wasting my time. I even pleaded the Trespass Offering, but it was no good." That is how solemn this matter is.

We know that the Lord did some extraordinary things, as He did with Ananias and Sapphira, in the early days of the church; but the way you treat a chapel is not the way you can treat the church. The way you treat some congregation of believers is not the way you can treat the body of the Lord Jesus Christ when it is an expression. All through church history, whenever the church has found some expression, however poor, men have withstood it or gainsaid it or argued with it. There has been the same thing. Read the stories of the Wesleys and Whitfields, or go back earlier to some of the Quaker times. You find it everywhere. The apostle says:

> ... to deliver such a one (a brother in the Lord) unto Satan
> for the destruction of the flesh, that the spirit may be
> saved in the day of the Lord Jesus. 1 Corinthians 5:5

Maybe you do not understand that, but let it be a sobering thought and let the fear of God come to you in this matter. Uncovering can lead to the destruction of the flesh, physically, that the spirit may be saved unto the day of Jesus Christ.

Ignorance of Satan's Devices

Let us come back from perhaps a more extreme uncovering such as that, to the more normal and general uncovering that most of us get into. We must say that so often, instead of heeding these solemn warnings and being alive to the danger, we are ignorant to Satan's devices and designs. We often say that it has happened before we know where we are. Before we know we are outside of Christ, it has happened. Even then, in many instances, I know of believers who do not know what has hit them. "Why? Why this? Why me? Why should it have happened?" Now of course, we have to be very careful when we speak like this; because the people who should not take this to heart, do, and the people who shake it all off are the people who should take it to heart. It is a most extraordinary thing. We have to be very careful or we find, suddenly, that folks who have got some inexplicable problem, which is a thorn in the flesh and has nothing to do with this matter at all but has come by sovereign and divine permission, suddenly begin to say, "Oh dear, oh dear, have I uncovered myself? Where have I done it?" Before we know where we are, this has happened and this is the whole problem. Surely, this is precisely why the Lord Jesus, in that pattern prayer in Matthew 6:9–13, taught us to pray that we should be kept covered.

> *Our Father which art in heaven, hallowed be thy name, thy*
> *kingdom come, thy will be done, on earth as it is in heaven.*
> *Give us this day our daily bread and forgive us our trespasses,*
> *as we forgive them that trespass against us. Lead us not*
> *into temptation, but deliver us from evil. Matthew 6:9–13*

In the Revised Standard Version and the American Standard Version, it is: "Lead us not into temptation, but deliver us from the evil one." The word temptation is trial or testing. "Oh Lord, do not bring us into a trial that will entice us in such a way that we get uncovered; but deliver us from the evil one." Do we pray enough in this way? Just because we know we are justified, just because we know we are absolutely safe in the Lord Jesus Christ, this is no reason for saying, "I do not need to pray anything like that." The Lord Jesus gave us a pattern prayer. He said when you pray, these are the essential things; and one of the things you must always remember to pray is: "Lead us not into temptation but deliver us from the evil one". I think that if such a consciousness of this danger came upon us, that every day of our lives we would pray this prayer: "Lord, now I am abiding; keep me abiding. Let an alarm bell ring in my spirit the moment I start to move out." This is what the Lord means. Pray along this line. Don't just take things for granted.

Ways to Get Uncovered

How then do we get uncovered? I think that is really the important question. I can only list some of the ways, which are representative of many others. The ways in which we can get uncovered are multitudinous. I can take just a number, and from these give you some understanding from the Word of God of how you get uncovered.

Not Walking in The Light

*And this is the message which we have heard from him
and announce unto you, that God is light, and in him*

is no darkness at all. If we say that we have fellowship
with him and walk in the darkness, we lie, and do not
the truth: but if we walk in the light, as he is in the light,
we have fellowship one with another, and the blood of
Jesus his Son cleanseth us from all sin. 1 John 1:5–7

We are to walk in the light with God as God is in the light; not according to our ideas, but according to His. If we walk in the light as He is in the light, it is objective, not subjective. It is not what I see as light so that I can say, "Well, I have not seen that." Walk in the light as God is in the light. The Book is your guide. You will see light in His light. "Walk in the light as He is in the light and the blood of Jesus Christ goes on cleansing you from all sin."

What happens if you do not walk in the light? There is no fellowship with God and no cleansing; you are uncovered. If communication with God is broken and you still go on thinking you have got it, you get into deception and from deception into bondage. He said: "If we walk in darkness and say we have fellowship with Him we lie and do not the truth." It is such a simple thing. Satan knows this very well. What does he do? He brings two people together who, at the beginning, are walking in the light. Then he brings up difficulties and before you know where you are, there is no more light. Things are being hidden, things are being buried, things are being pushed under the carpet; and the dust is being swept under there and put down. Something has happened. There is no more walking in the light. I know some people who are afraid to go to certain meetings or even hear certain speakers. Why is this if we are walking in the light as He is in the light? Something intuitively tells you if God meets you in this, it will break you. So you go back from the light and, without knowing it, you are uncovered. Instead of walking, instead of a progress in light, there is a deterioration into darkness.

The only way you can get more light is to obey the light God has given you. That is a law of fellowship with God. How do you get uncovered? God puts His finger on something in your life and you say, "No". God puts His finger the third time upon it, and you say, "No". God does not do it again—sometimes He does, sometimes He doesn't. From that point, there is darkness. You can sing the hymns, you can read the Bible; and those who do not have any discernment will still think you are going on full steam. But those who have any spiritual discernment at all will note that something is being turned off. "Walking in the light as He is in the light." Do not, for God's sake, shrug off such a thing as this! Think to yourself what the Word of God says: "If we walk in the light as He is in the light we have fellowship one with another and the blood of Jesus Christ, God's Son cleanses us from all sin.

An Unforgiving Spirit

This does not mean believers only, but it is forgiveness for any human being. Think again of the pattern prayer: "Forgive us our trespasses as we forgive them that trespass against us." Why did the Lord do that? He taught us to pray: "Forgive us as ..." In other words, if there is someone I cannot forgive, dead or alive, I get uncovered.

Wherefore I beseech you to confirm your love toward
him, for to this end also did I write, that I might know the

proof of you, whether ye are obedient in all things. But
to whom ye forgive anything, I forgive also: for what I
also have forgiven, if I have forgiven anything, for your
sakes have I forgiven it in the presence of Christ; that no
advantage may be gained over us by Satan: for we are
not ignorant of his devices. II Corinthians 2:8–11

Have you ever noticed this: "... that no advantage might be
gained over us by Satan, for we are not ignorant of his devices"?
Even the apostle says, "This man whom I have delivered to Satan
for the destruction of the flesh, I forgive. Now that he has repented,
I forgive. You forgive and I forgive; because if I don't forgive, Satan
will get an advantage and there will be uncovering. We are not
ignorant of his devices." Some of the modern versions say "his
designs", but it is the same idea behind it of what Satan is up to.

Do you remember the story in Matthew 18 about the two
debtors, one who had so much and the man who had very little?
The master forgave the man who owed so much, but that one
would not forgive someone else who owed very little to him.
He was prepared to really put the pressure on him; and so the
master said, "Throw him into jail. He shall stay in jail until he has
paid every single penny."

So shall also my heavenly Father do unto you, if ye forgive
not every one his brother from your hearts. Matthew 18:35

Some of us have parents we cannot forgive; some of us have
children we cannot forgive; some of us have relatives we cannot
forgive; some of us have bosses we cannot forgive; and we have no

idea that this unforgiveness is getting us uncovered. Inextricably, we have been pushed out of our position in Christ by our unforgiving spirit. Unless God can get us through on this thing and give us such a revelation of His forgiveness to us that we can forgive; unless we can forgive as He forgave us, we will be out. We will no longer be hid with Christ in God.

Not Loving One Another

Maybe you have never thought that just by this simple way of not loving one another, we get uncovered. Of course, it has to do with not forgiving.

He that loveth his brother abideth in the light, and there is no occasion of stumbling in him. 1 John 2:10 ASV

He who loves his brother abides in the light and in it there is no cause for stumbling. 1 John 2:10 RSV

The man who loves his brother lives and moves in the light and has no reason to stumble. 1 John 2:10 Phillips

Only the man who loves his brother dwells in light. There is nothing to make him stumble. 1 John 2:10 New English Bible

If I do not love my brother, I am not dwelling in the light, and I am uncovered. I shall stumble, and I shall fall. Is this why, so often, many believers fall? When we first become children of God, we love all the saints. We think they are the most sweet, godly, innocent lot that we have ever set our eyes upon; but when we get to know them, the shocks we have, the disappointments we have, the disillusionments and betrayals that we have. We are let down until, in the end, we wonder, "Can I love? Can I love?" But if we do not love our brother or sister we are out from covering. Again, it is an absolute law. The moment I no longer love, in that moment, I am pushed out of my position in Christ.

An Untamed Tongue

Speak not one against another, brethren. He that speaketh against a brother, or judgeth his brother, speaketh against the law, and judgeth the law: but if thou judgest the law, thou art not a doer of the law, but a judge. One only is the lawgiver and judge, even he who is able to save and to destroy: but who art thou that judgest thy neighbor? James 4:11–12

For the whole law is fulfilled in one word, even in this: Thou shalt love thy neighbor as thyself. But if ye bite and devour one another, take heed that ye be not consumed one of another. Galatians 5:14–15

There is uncovering. Can any Christian be consumed? Yes! If we bite and devour one another by the kind of loose talk we can indulge in–backchat, chitchat, talebearing, whispering, and all this kind of thing–we are in danger of being consumed. The thing will come back like a boomerang, a great backwash that will consume us. I have seen it happen again and again–a backwash which has come and swamped the person concerned. There is a tremendous amount in this matter of the tongue.

*For in many things we all stumble. If any stumbleth
not in word, the same is a perfect man, able to
bridle the whole body also. James 3:2*

*But the tongue can no man tame; it is a restless evil,
it is full of deadly poison. Therewith bless we the
Lord and Father; and therewith curse we men, who
are made after the likeness of God. James 3:8–9*

It is a sobering thought that this is addressed to believers. James goes on in the next chapter and says: "Speak not one against another brethren." This tongue with which we bless God, sing His praises, read His Word, and pray is the same tongue we can use against one another. But it is not only against one another we can use the tongue; we can use the tongue against the Lord and not even know it. Again and again, we can say things about the work of God which Satan hears. People say, "Ahh, but God knows my heart." Yes, but the same God who knows your heart said: "By every word that proceedeth out of your mouth shall you be judged" (Matthew 12:37). "Out of the abundance of the heart the mouth speaketh" (Matthew 12:34). God does not just look upon the heart and say, "Oh, it is all right." God knows very well the kind of thing that comes out of the mouth is like a little straw which shows which way the wind is blowing. "The tongue can no man tame."

I think that of all the ways in which we get uncovered, the tongue is one of the major causes. Sometimes, I have nearly bitten my tongue. You say something before you know it and you just feel dirty. "Oh, I feel dirty. I am uncovered. I should not have said that." Sometimes, you listen to someone else telling you something about another believer and you know in your heart you ought to say, "I do not want to hear it"; but you listen, and afterwards you feel dirty. You are uncovered because you have not disassociated yourself. You have become a partaker with that sin and you are unclean; you are uncovered.

Sometimes, we can talk so inadvisably about the work of God, the will of God, or the purpose of God. I think about years ago when people said things about the way we were going, the will of God, the purpose of God. They laughed at it; they derided it. They told us that we were fools and had big ideas, thinking we were going places; and all that kind of thing. God taught us some lessons: do not argue, do not get involved, keep your mouth closed. And where are they? God said, "You shall look for them and you shall not find them." It is absolutely true; not one of them can we find. When we take on something, God leaves us to fight it out; but when someone speaks against us or says things against us and we leave it to the Lord, He takes it on.

He that guardeth his mouth keepeth his life. Proverbs 13:3

Don't you know many people who do not guard their lips and they have still got their life? No, it does not mean that. It means he that guardeth his mouth keepeth his soul in life. "But he that openeth wide his lips shall have destruction." Uncovering! A person who opens their mouth and just says everything gets uncovered; it is destruction.

Who so keepeth his mouth and his tongue keepeth
his soul from troubles. Proverbs 21:23

The one who watches his mouth and his tongue keeps covered.
He that hath a wayward heart findeth no good; And he that
hath a perverse tongue falleth into mischief. Proverbs 17:20

Dear child of God, how easily this little tongue, that no man can tame, can get us uncovered. We can say things about a message we have heard; we can say things about someone else's way with God; we can say things about a company; we can say things about a work of God. I have heard things said that I have trembled for; because it is so possible to say something inadvisably with the lips and uncover yourself. Without knowing it, you are opposing God and God has heard. If God hears the conversations of those that fear His name and writes them in a book, will He not also hear the conversations of those who speak inadvisably with their lips? It is not just that God wants to cause trouble or be severe, but we have an enemy. He is an enemy who listens to everything, who picks up so many things and goes into the presence of God and says, "So-and-so said so-and- so." Uncovering!

We all have this tongue; and it is a comfort, in one way, that the Lord has said: "The tongue can no man tame." He says every beast is tameable, but not the tongue. But God can do the impossible. He can tame the tongue. He can teach us how to get those inner frustrations, that so often come out in our words, dealt with; how those deep roots of bitterness can be pulled out. He can show us how we can positively experience all that God has given us in Christ.

How do we get uncovered? If only it was just a simple matter of not claiming the blood of Christ, as some people think; if only it was a simple matter of defaming the name of the Lord; but getting uncovered is a complex matter. There are multitudes of ways in which we can do it and only God can show us.

Christ Makes Intercession for Us

Finally, let us be positive. There is absolute safety for us in the Lord Jesus Christ. We should never forget that the Lord Jesus ever lives to make intercession for us. When we have used our lips inadvisably, when there is an unforgiving spirit, when we cannot love someone as we ought, when our tongues run away with us, the Lord is praying. He said of Peter, who got himself uncovered, and the other eleven: "Satan has obtained you by request that he might sift you as wheat, but I have prayed for you that your faith fail not." They got uncovered and Satan had come in; but the Lord Jesus was interceding that they might come through. Thank God for the ministry of the Lord Jesus Christ who sees our situation much better than we do, who understands us much more deeply and fully than we understand ourselves, who loves us with a love that is stronger than death, and who ever lives to make intercession!

Who shall lay anything to the charge of God's
elect? It is God that justifieth. Romans 8:33

Let us pray:

Lord, we commit ourselves to Thee. We pray that Thou will not allow this study to be just negative, just one that may be somewhat frightening; but we pray that, positively, we may all know what it is to enjoy absolute safety in the Lord Jesus Christ and to know that in Him we must overcome. Lord, show this to everyone of us we pray— where we have got ourselves uncovered and when we get ourselves uncovered—how to get back quickly. Dear Lord, write this message in our heart. We ask it in the name of our Lord Jesus. Amen.

4.
The Danger of Getting Uncovered–Part Two

John 17:1–26

These things spake Jesus; and lifting up his eyes to heaven, he said, Father, the hour is come; glorify thy Son, that the Son may glorify thee: even as thou gavest him authority over all flesh, that to all whom thou hast given him, he should give eternal life. And this is life eternal, that they should know thee the only true God, and him whom thou didst send, even Jesus Christ. I glorified thee on the earth, having accomplished the work which thou hast given me to do. And now, Father, glorify thou me with thine own self with the glory which I had with thee before the world was. I manifested thy name unto the men whom thou gavest me out of the world: thine they were, and thou gavest them to me; and they have kept thy word. Now they know that all things whatsoever thou hast given me are from thee: for the words which thou gavest me I have given unto them; and they received them, and knew of a truth that I came forth from thee, and they believed that thou didst send me. I pray for them: I pray not for the world, but for those whom thou hast given me; for they are thine: and all things that are mine are thine, and thine are mine: and I am glorified in them. And I am no more in the world, and these are in the world, and I come to thee. Holy Father, keep them in thy name which thou hast given me, that they may be one, even as we are. While I was with them, I kept them in thy name which thou hast given me: and I guarded them, and not one of them perished, but the son of perdition; that the scripture might be fulfilled. But now I come to thee; and these things I speak in the world, that they may have my joy made full in themselves. I have given them thy word; and the world hated them, because they are not of the world, even as I am not of the world. I pray not that thou shouldest take them from the world, but that thou shouldest keep them from the evil one. They are not of the world, even as I am not of the world. Sanctify them in the truth: thy word is truth. As thou didst send me into the world, even so sent I them into the world. And for their sakes I sanctify myself, that they themselves also may be sanctified in truth. Neither for these only do I pray, but for them also that believe on me through their word; that they may all be one; even as thou, Father, art in me, and I in thee, that they also may be in us: that the world may believe that thou didst send me. And the glory which thou hast given me I have given unto them; that they may be one, even as we are one; I in them, and thou in me, that they may be perfected into one; that the world may know that *thou didst send me, and lovedst them, even as thou lovedst me. Father, I desire that they also whom thou hast given me be with me where I am, that they may behold my glory, which thou hast given me: for thou lovedst me before the foundation of the world. O righteous Father, the world knew thee not, but I knew thee; and these knew that thou didst send me; and I made known unto them thy name, and will make it known; that the love wherewith thou lovedst me may be in them, and I in them.*

Shall we pray?

Beloved Lord, Thou alone knowest the mystery of this whole matter. Once more we acknowledge it before Thee and know that nothing less than the ministry of Thy Holy Spirit can enable speaker or hearer to discover, dear Lord, all that Thou art for us. Oh, may it be so this time. We ask it in the name of our Lord Jesus. Amen.

We have been considering this matter of the danger of getting uncovered. We pointed out that Satan has one over-all objective upon which he bases his whole strategy, and that is to get the believer or the church uncovered. He, more than anyone else, knows that the believer is absolutely safe while in Christ. Satan knows he must first meet with Christ before he can get at the believer. He knows that while the believer is in Christ and abiding in Christ, "hid with Christ in God", he cannot reach that one. He knows that while the church is in Christ, its life "hid with

Christ in God", he cannot reach the life of the church except by first meeting God. Therefore, his whole plan is to entice us out, by one means or another to get us to uncover ourselves, to bring us out from abiding in Christ, and to draw us away from our position in Him.

The ways in which we can get uncovered are multitudinous. Therefore, we are just selecting a few that are representative of many more. We have already dealt with four; so we will take up the next one.

Being Proud

Of all the causes of getting uncovered, I do not think there is any one which is a more basic and primary cause than pride. It lies behind quite a few of these other things that we will be mentioning later, and some that we have already mentioned.

> *Thou wast the anointed cherub that covereth: and I*
> *set thee, so that thou wast upon the holy mountain*
> *of God; thou hast walked up and down in the*
> *midst of the stones of fire. Ezekiel 28:14*

> *Thy heart was lifted up because of thy beauty;*
> *thou hast corrupted thy wisdom by reason*
> *of thy brightness. Ezekiel 28:17*

This is speaking of Satan who fell through pride. Compare this with Isaiah 14:12–15, which again has to do with Lucifer, son of the morning. He said: "I will exalt my throne to the throne of

God. I will be like the Most High." Pride was the first real cause of uncovering. Pride is the thing that unfailingly brings us into uncovering. If we are not walking in the light, so often it is because pride lies at the root of it. Sometimes, the fact that we cannot forgive a person is due to hurt pride. Presumption in the presence of God is pride. The arrogating to ourselves of a position which is not ours spiritually is pride. So much stems from this one thing.

But He Giveth More Grace

Wherefore the scripture saith, God resisteth the proud, but giveth grace to the humble. Be subject therefore unto God; but resist the devil, and he will flee from you. James 4:6–7

When pride is found in us, even when we are not conscious of it, God resists us. Could there be any clearer indication of getting uncovered than when God turns around and becomes our resister instead of our protector? He resists the proud, but those that humble themselves know grace. If we are subject unto God, we humble ourselves. We can resist the devil and he flees from us. There is covering for you! You stand in the Lord and withstand; and having done all, you stand.

Pride goeth before destruction. And a haughty spirit before a fall. Proverbs 16:18

This is spoken to us as believers. "Pride goeth before destruction and a haughty spirit before a fall." Is there anything any clearer than the fact that we can get uncovered through pride? Oh, the need for us to know the brokenness of the cross; the need for us to know that continual work of God keeping us low. So often we can say things, we can do things, we can take positions or we can take attitudes; but behind it all lies pride.

Before destruction the heart of man is haughty; And before honor goeth humility. Proverbs 18:12

For thus saith the high and lofty One that inhabiteth eternity, whose name is Holy: I dwell in the high and holy place, with him also that is of a contrite and humble spirit, to revive the spirit of the humble, and to revive the heart of the contrite. Isaiah 57:15

For all these things hath my hand made, and so all these things came to be, saith the Lord: but to this man will I look, even to him that is poor and of a contrite spirit, and that trembleth at my word. Isaiah 66:2

There is no arrogance there, no seizing hold of the Lord's words and saying, "Now I will pass it on." The man trembles at the Word of God.

Not Fearing the Lord

This is very much wrapped up with the question of pride. All of these are interlocked or interwoven. "He that trembleth at my Word" is the opposite of pride. "No fear of the Lord" means there is no trembling at His Word; no sensitive awareness of its solemnity; no sensitive, practical awareness of what it means to be in a living relationship with God, Himself, through the Lord Jesus Christ.

> *Wherefore, receiving a kingdom that cannot be shaken,*
> (there is our covering) *let us have grace whereby we may*
> *offer service well-pleasing to God with reverence and awe:*
> *for our God is a consuming fire. Hebrews 12:28–29*

This is spoken to believers. I doubt whether many of us understand that God is a consuming fire. This God of all grace, this God whose arms are open to returning sinners, this God whose second name is Mercy, "is a consuming fire", says the writer of this tremendous letter. "Let us offer service that is well-pleasing to God with reverence in the fear of the Lord and awe, for our God is a consuming fire." He has not changed from the Old Testament. I is still I AM.

> *If thou wilt not observe to do all the words of this law*
> *that are written in this book, that thou mayest fear this*
> *glorious and fearful name, the LORD THY GOD; then*
> *the Lord will make thy plagues of thy seed, even great*
> *plagues, and of long continuance, and sore sicknesses, and*
> *of long continuance. And he will bring upon thee again*
> *all the diseases of Egypt, which thou wast afraid of; and*
> *they shall cleave unto thee. Also every sickness, and every*
> *plague, which is not written in the book of this law, them will*
> *the Lord bring upon thee, until thou be destroyed. And ye*
> *shall be left few in number, whereas ye were as the stars of*

heaven for multitude; because thou didst not hearken unto the voice of the Lord thy God. Deuteronomy 28:58–62

Well; by their unbelief they were broken off, and thou standest by thy faith. Be not high-minded, but fear: for if God spared not the natural branches, neither will he spare thee. Romans 11:20–21

Come, ye children, hearken unto me: I will teach you the fear of the Lord. What man is he that desireth life, and loveth many days, that he may see good? Keep thy tongue from evil, and thy lips from speaking guile. Depart from evil, and do good; seek peace, and pursue it. Psalm 34:11–14

The fear of the Lord is clean, enduring for ever: The ordinances of the Lord are true, and righteous altogether. Psalm 19:9

Isn't that an extraordinary statement? Of all the things to talk about concerning the fear of the Lord, I would have least thought of this: "The fear of the Lord is clean." That is because natural fear is often dirty. There is some sting in it; there is a torment in it; it comes from the pit, from Satan. But "the fear of the Lord is clean, enduring for ever." What does it mean "enduring for ever"? Does it only mean that the fear of the Lord is something that goes on forever just because He is I AM; and therefore, we shall always fear Him, being sensitively aware and reverent in our dealing with Him? Don't you think it also means "the fear of the Lord is clean" causing us to endure forever? It brings something enduring into us.

I think of Ananias and Sapphira as examples of those who did not fear the Lord. If you want to understand what the fear of the Lord is or what it is not, look at Ananias and Sapphira. What did they do? What they did was quite simple. They sold all of their property. But when they brought the money to the disciples, they said it was all the money from the sale of the property; whereas, in actual fact, they had kept part of the money for themselves. Don't you think many of us have done that kind of thing? How many people have said, "Lord, I have given you everything"? For Ananias and Sapphira, there was no fear of the Lord. They thought they were dealing with human leaders. "Dear old Peter, he is a lovely man—a fisherman. With his background, we can pull the wool over his eyes. We are land owners; we are a little bit more shrewd. All we have to do is go in and say, 'Well, Peter, here is the money. We have sold all our property and we want to make it all a gift to the work of God.' And John is so poetic; a charming, younger man. He is one of those dreamy types, always meditating, always seeing visions. We can pull the wool over his eyes. Then there is the church—marvelous crowd. We were there on the day of Pentecost. It was terrific. You should have heard them. It was absolutely marvelous."

Peter said to them, "Do you not fear the Lord that you have lied to the Holy Ghost?" They may well have said, if they had gotten the chance before they died, "But Lord, we have never lied to the Holy Ghost. We are dealing with frail human beings like ourselves." "Oh no," God says, "you forget Peter and John; you are dealing with Me. You forget the church and all its frail vessels; you are dealing with Me. You have lied to the Holy Ghost!" Ananias fell down. His wife came in as he was being taken out and she repeated the whole procedure. They had evidently agreed together. It was a premeditated thing to take in the church. Now that is what it is to have no fear of the Lord.

Some people think that to have no fear of the Lord means you are just presumptuous in your dealings directly with Him. Very few Christians are ever presumptuous directly in their dealings with God, although I have heard some. But it is in our dealings with one another this occurs; because without even realizing it, we are dealing with the Lord. One theologian once said: "If God had dealt with all believers as drastically as He dealt with Ananias and Sapphira, he reckoned about seventy percent of the church would be dead." It is the mercy of the Lord that He has not, but the principle always remains. We may not physically die, although in some cases we may. But always there comes spiritual paralysis and bondage if there is no fear of the Lord.

Taking The Name of the Lord in Vain

Thou shalt not take the name of the Lord thy God in vain; for the Lord will not hold him guiltless that taketh his name in vain. Exodus 20:7

The New English Bible puts it like this: "You shall not make wrong use of the name of the Lord your God. The Lord will not leave unpunished the man who misuses His name." That is an abiding principle when you take the name of the Lord in vain. What does it mean "in vain"? It means in a false way or in an empty way.

After this manner therefore pray ye, Our Father who
art in heaven, Hallowed be thy name. Matthew 6:9

Have you ever thought of that? The Lord Jesus taught us, as soon as we open our mouths with God, to remember the Name: "Hallowed be thy name". What does this word hallowed mean? It means "to make holy" or "to sanctify". It means to make His name the opposite of common. Some of us can make the name of the Lord common. We can so devalue the name of the Lord that it becomes common coinage. Don't take the name of the Lord in vain.

What does it mean to take the name of the Lord in vain? "The Lord told me to do so-and-so." The Lord has never said a thing. Oh, how common it is to say, "The Lord told me." And the Lord says, "I know nothing of it." The name of the Lord has been taken in vain. Now when the Lord tells you something, you say it humbly: "The Lord has given me this." Sometimes, we get up and say, "The Lord has given me a word"; and the Lord says, "I have given no such word." Sometimes, a person uses a gift in the wrong way and then says the Lord told them. But the Lord says, "You have taken my name in vain; I never said anything of the kind." It is the wrong use of the name of the Lord. Don't we all fail here? Is there one of us that has not taken the name of the Lord in vain in some way or another? That is why we need to know how to get recovered when we do this, because it is one of the surest ways to uncover ourselves.

It is so possible to tack the name of the Lord on to something to justify our course of action, to justify ourselves in front of others, without realizing that we are not hallowing the name of the Lord but making it common. We are devaluing it into a tool so that we can impress others, so that we can get our own way with the church, so that we can somehow make some impact on others. It is to take the name of the Lord in vain, and in that moment we are uncovered. Instead of the name of the Lord being a high tower or a strong tower into which the righteous run and is safe, it becomes the exact opposite. Our misuse of it means that we are driven out.

I have heard it said in some quarters that referring to our Lord Jesus as Lord Jesus is a lot of traditional nonsense and that we should speak to Him as Jesus. In many places, the name of Jesus is chanted like Hindus or Moslems chant. There are other people who address the Lord or speak of Him in such a way that you think He is completely devalued. Let me tell you some facts about His name. The name, Jesus, is used six hundred fifty-one times in the New Testament–five hundred ninety-four times in the four gospels, and only fifty-seven times in the rest of the New Testament from Acts to Revelation.

Christ or Jesus Christ is used four hundred eight times–fifty-six times only in the four gospels and three hundred fifty-two times from Acts to Revelation. The term or title Lord or Lord Jesus or Lord Jesus Christ is used three hundred sixty-four times in the New Testament–one hundred twenty- six times only in the four gospels and two hundred thirty-eight times from Acts to Revelation. All this proves that the very apostles who spoke to the Lord Jesus as "Jesus", after His ascension began to speak of Him as the "Lord Jesus" or "Jesus our Lord". We must be very careful of how we take the name of our Lord. People seem to think that if they just say the name "Jesus, Jesus, Jesus", it will charm the devil away. Far from it, if it is the taking of the name of the Lord in vain. We need to take very careful note of this.

> *Then they that feared the Lord spake one with another;*
> *and the Lord hearkened, and heard, and a book of*
> *remembrance was written before him, for them that feared*
> *the Lord, and that thought upon his name. Malachi 3:16*

These people that feared the Lord thought upon His name. Isn't that amazing? What does it mean? This little remnant was so sensitively aware of God that they thought upon His name; and it was so singular, so unique, so precious to God, that He recorded their conversations.

> *But the prophet, that shall speak a word presumptuously*
> *in my name, which I have not commanded him to speak,*
> *or that shall speak in the name of other gods, that same*
> *prophet shall die. And if thou say in thy heart, How shall*
> *we know the word which the Lord hath not spoken? When a*
> *prophet speaketh in the name of the Lord, if the thing follow*
> *not, nor come to pass, that is the thing which the Lord hath*
> *not spoken: the prophet hath spoken it presumptuously,*
> *thou shalt not be afraid of him. Deuteronomy 18:20–22*

That is very, very severe, isn't it? Anyone that stands up and speaks in the name of the Lord and it is not in the name of the Lord shall die. That was the old covenant. How serious it is to take the name of the Lord in vain!

Making Presumptuous Claims

Simon, Simon, behold, Satan asked to have you, that he might
sift you as wheat: but I made supplication for thee, that thy
faith fail not; and do thou, when once thou hast turned again,
establish thy brethren. And he said unto him, Lord, with thee
I am ready to go both to prison and to death. And he said, I
tell thee, Peter, the cock shall not crow this day, until thou
shalt thrice deny that thou knowest me. Luke 22:31–34

In the Authorized version or one of the modern versions, you will
see that the "you" in verse 31 is plural and the "you" in verse 32
is singular. That is why in the Authorized version, it is: "Simon,
Simon, Satan has desired to have you. I have prayed for thee that
thy faith fail not." Phillips puts it like this: "Oh, Simon, Simon,
do you know that Satan has asked to have you all to sift you like
wheat but I have prayed for you that your faith fail not." The New
English Bible puts it: "Simon, Simon, take heed, Satan has been
given leave to sift all of you like wheat, but for you I have prayed
that your faith may not fail." Presumptuous claims!

And Jesus saith unto them, All ye shall be offended: for it
is written, I will smite the shepherd, and the sheep shall be
scattered abroad. Howbeit, after I am raised up, I will go
before you into Galilee. But Peter said unto him, Although
all shall be offended, yet will not I. And Jesus saith unto
him, Verily I say unto thee, that thou today, even this night,
before the cock crow twice, shalt deny me thrice. But he spake

exceeding vehemently, If I must die with thee, I will not deny thee. And in like manner also said they all. Mark 14:27–31

So often poor old Peter gets the blame for something that the whole lot said. He was, in fact, just the spokesman for the whole lot. He said, "I am prepared to die with you, Lord." That was his claim; that was his testimony. "I am prepared to die for the Lord, come what may." Thank God when we can say it and it comes out of deep history and deep experiences with God; but you see what happens when it is a presumptuous claim. "Satan has obtained leave to have you all." They all said the same thing; and Satan hurried into the presence of God and said, "Now then, they have all said they will die for the Lord Jesus." Of course, you know what happened. Everyone of them failed, but something came through because the Lord Jesus had prayed for each one. When He said, "I prayed for you, Peter", it did not mean that He had not prayed for the others. It is quite clear that in Gethsemane He prayed for them all, one by one. Isn't it lovely? It is personal. "I prayed for you, personally, by name." Peter had gotten uncovered; they had all become uncovered; but the Lord Jesus knew about it and had prayed for them.

Keep thy foot when thou goest to the house of God; for to draw nigh to hear is better than to give the sacrifice of fools: for they know not that they do evil. Be not rash with thy mouth, and let not thy heart be hasty to utter anything before God; for God is in heaven, and thou upon earth: therefore let thy words be few. Ecclesiastes 5:1–2

This is rather sobering; but it is not meant to stop us from saying anything to the Lord when it is real and upon us, but rather to think it out. Don't just suddenly make vows rashly, because it is no good saying, "But God knew my heart". What has been uttered with the mouth has gone out and there are other forces that hear it.

> *It is a snare to a man rashly to say, It is holy, And*
> *after vows to make inquiry. Proverbs 20:25*

The New English Bible puts it like this: "It is dangerous to dedicate a gift rashly or to make a vow and have second thoughts." My! That finds me out. It is dangerous to make a vow and have second thoughts. It is better not to have made the vow. I have seen many go off the rails in this matter. We can do it so easily in testimony; we can do it so easily in dealings with one another, especially when we get heated. We start to make presumptuous claims. We can do it easily in other ways. Pride is the root of it. Oh, that God would guard us!

Calling Satan Names

> *But Michael the archangel, when contending with the*
> *devil he disputed about the body of Moses, durst not bring*
> *against him a railing judgment, but said, The Lord rebuke*
> *thee. But these rail at whatsoever things they know not: and*
> *what they understand naturally, like the creatures without*
> *reason, in these things are they destroyed. Jude 9–10*

Never call Satan names. Never make a joke about Satan. Never try to denigrate Satan. Be very, very careful; Satan is a terrible reality. Even the archangel, Michael, durst not bring a railing accusation against him, let alone call him names. He did not dare say, "You so-and-so; you are doing so-and-so." He did not dare do it, but said: "The Lord rebuke thee, Satan."

Some years ago, I remember a prayer meeting over a particular sister in great need. She was very, very unwell mentally. One of the brothers, who was always known for being rather forward and rather too quick for always jumping in at the beginning and always contributing, suddenly jumped up and said: "You slimy serpent Satan, get out of her!" and a few other things. It was like an electric shock for me. I knew he was finished, absolutely finished. He thought he was doing the work of God and warring with Satan, but I knew he was finished. I prayed halfheartedly, "Oh God, cover us." All of us had prayed, but I knew it was not understood. He thought the others did not have the power to deal with this situation. That night a curtain came down and never lifted until many, many years later. About three years ago, the curtain lifted when he got it all right with God. Satan had him for year after year in absolute, total darkness. He could not worship, he could not pray, he could not even read his Bible, he could not go to church, he could not do anything.

Do you honestly think you can call Satan names and get away with it? Today, it is fashionable to call all those with any authority or any power names, or to think we can answer them back; but in spiritual things, we cannot get away with it. We live in days when dignitaries are railed at. Sometimes, they deserve it. But the fact of the matter is that in these anti-authoritarian days in which we live, let us not think that we can just do anything with Satan. This does not mean that we don't stand up, we don't resist the devil; but it is the way we do it: "The Lord rebuke you, Satan."

I could give you many more instances of this kind of thing. I remember a dear man whose little son was desperately ill. He had this idea that all sickness was due to sin and that you should be healed willy-nilly. He went into the presence of God, and first of all, he tried to shake the Lord like a rat. That is the only word for it. He said: "Oh God, if you don't heal my baby, you are a liar." You cannot do that kind of thing, but who had the courage to say that to a demented father? Then he turned on Satan and called him a hound and a swine and told him to get out of that house. That night his son died. You cannot do these kinds of things. You cannot call Satan names and get away with it. Even the greatest figure in the angelic hosts, Michael, durst not bring a railing accusation against him; but he hid in the Lord by saying, "The Lord rebuke thee".

Mrs. Penn-Lewis once said that whenever dealing with evil spirits, try to keep the "I" out of it. Never say, "I command you to get out in the name of Jesus Christ"; but say, "We". Hide in the church, in Christ, because from bitter experience, those who know the most have discovered that the forces of darkness can hit back if there is any uncovering.

Not Heeding and Obeying the Anointing

And as for you, the anointing which ye received of him abideth in you, and ye need not that any one teach you; but as his

anointing teacheth you concerning all things, and is true, and
is no lie, and even as it taught you, ye abide in him. 1 John 2:27

As long as we listen to the anointing within us telling us what is right and what is wrong, we are abiding in Him. But the moment we do not heed the anointing, we become uncovered; we are no longer abiding. That is the seriousness of this question of the anointing. Again, we have found that in our experience. There are times when we have felt very unhappy about a particular ministry or particular movement and we have sort of beaten ourselves and wondered, "Oh, are we being unkind, is it because we won't surrender, are we not prepared to go forward with God," and all the rest of it. Finally, we have given in and gone on to find that we have gone out of our position in Christ. We are uncovered. Whenever you have that warning bell in your spirit, heed it, and you will stay under covering.

Committing Habitual and Willful Sin

If a person thinks that he can do something really sinful, grossly evil and wicked, and just claim the blood of the Lamb every time he does it and go on, that person is mistaken.

> *For if we sin wilfully after that we have received*
> *the knowledge of the truth, there remaineth no*
> *more a sacrifice for sins. Hebrews 10:26*

God does not become party to our deception. I remember sometime ago a person came to me who was in terrible need.

He was doing something which was criminal, but he said to me, "But you see, I know the love of God and every time I do it I say, 'Lord, forgive me.'" And I said to him, "But the Lord has not forgiven you." He was messing up his daughters' lives, destroying them and thinking that God would forgive him. "For such there remaineth no more sacrifice for sins, but a fearful looking toward judgment." You cannot play with something like that. I said to him, "Come to the brothers and ask for help." "Oh no!" and he was out. He would not share it with anyone. He would not bring it out into the light. It took him months before he brought it out into the light with me.

Being Disobedient

There is general disobedience, which is not keeping His commandments; or, in particular, disobeying what His will is for me.

> Look therefore carefully how ye walk, not as unwise,
> but as wise; redeeming the time, because the days
> are evil. Wherefore be ye not foolish, but understand
> what the will of the Lord is. Ephesians 5:15–17

We need to be kept in the will of God. May I give you an illustration of this:

> Let us therefore give diligence to enter into that rest, that no
> man fall after the same example of disobedience. Hebrews 4:11

The will of God was that they should enter into the land and take it. If we are disobedient, we fall.

*Let us fear therefore, lest haply, a promise being
left of entering into his rest, any one of you should
seem to have come short of it. Hebrews 4:1*

*And to whom sware he that they should not enter into his
rest, but to them that were disobedient? Hebrews 3:18*

Disobedience is one of the real causes of getting uncovered. I know people whom God had His hand on for service when I was younger. Some of them were disobedient and now they are right in the far country. One girl I can think of is a bar lady. She used to be a Sunday School teacher in a keen evangelical church. She thought God had called her to His work, and I think He had; but she was disobedient. Uncovering. Sometimes on the smallest issues of obedience or disobedience, there rests a tremendous amount.

Setting Aside Divine Order

We find Scripture for this in 1 Peter 2:13 to 3:7 and 5:1–8. God has divine order that is divine order, and this is true in every single sphere. There is divine order in my personal life. God is first, absolutely first; then the people of God; others are next. "Thou shall love the Lord thy God with all thy soul, thy neighbor as thyself." This is divine order. If we change that divine order, we can get ourselves uncovered. In other words, if I refuse to accept the Lord Jesus Christ as my Lord, I can get uncovered. It goes back to the question of the will of God. If He cannot direct me into His will because I have not made Him Lord, I have set aside divine order and I get uncovered.

Divine order is in every sphere, even society. We are told that the magistrate is as God to us; we are told to honor the king; we are told to pray for those in authority; we are told to be subject to every ordinance of man for the Lord's sake. There is divine order. No Christian can simply go against things just like that. Now there are times when we have to vote against things, and there are times when, perhaps, we have to go even further than that; otherwise, there would have been no progress. But be very careful that it is not just the spirit of the age that is in us against the government.

There is divine order in the church, and if you read those first eight verses of I Peter 5, you find it there. If I set it aside and set myself up as an authority, then immediately, I am uncovered. "Obey them that have the rule over you," it says in Scripture. That is one thing. Then it speaks of them that have the rule that they should not be, as J. B. Phillips puts it, "Little tin gods lording it over the flock". They should care for the flock, love the flock, lay down their lives for the flock. There is a divine order; everyone has got a place. God has set in the church some and some and some and some. We cannot set it aside. We may think God has made a mess of it. So-and-so should be there; this should be; that should be. Be careful that we don't set aside divine order without even knowing it. In the Old Testament, we find illustration after illustration of this truth–those that thought they knew better than God. Of course, they did not put it like that. They just thought that the kind of human beings they were up against could be bettered, but they came up against God. There is divine order.

In the family, there is divine order. We live in days of women's lib; but women's lib does not necessarily mean that God approves. We do not mean at all that ladies are inferior to gentlemen. Far from it! They may, in fact, be greatly superior; but there is a divine order. Why is it that the apostle, writing one of his greatest letters, takes over one third of it dealing with matters in the church, relationships in the church, divine order (if you like); and then husbands and wives, wives and husbands, parents and children, children and parents, employers and employees, and employees and employers? Why not just simply say, "Now then everyone live under the government of God fullstop. We live in these wonderful days of the freedom of the spirit when everyone can do what is right, what he feels to be the way of God for him. And if we all do what we feel to be the way of God for us, we shall not clash but all harmonize." He could have saved a whole chapter by using that one verse or two. Instead, we have this tremendous amount of instruction; and Colossians is the same and the Apostle Peter does the same in the passages I have given you and so it goes on. Why are all these so concerned? It is because they are up against divine order. It is not a question of inequality; it is a question of divine order. We all have a place to fill and a part to play. If one tries to do the other's job and that one the other's, it is against divine order. Some folks will immediately say, "Oh dear, we will get into bondage over this kind of thing." No, you won't! All it means is this: if a wife starts bossing a husband around, she gets uncovered. That is putting it in bold twentieth century language. When you go around in the Lord's work, you see some incredible things. I have seen husbands wrung out like dishcloths by their wives, even in front of the visiting preacher. Maybe it was justified, but there is one thing you can be sure of–uncovering comes with misery and darkness. It is the other way around, too. If husbands just put up with their wives, instead of loving them, you get uncovering.

The Apostle Peter says, "... that your prayers be not hindered" (1 Peter 3:7). Isn't that an extraordinary statement? It is in that passage about not having braided hair or gold jewels or apparel. Some people think that this means ladies should never braid their hair or never have a bit of jewelry on any part of their being. But may I ask what we do with apparel? Obviously, they are not to be unapparelled. It does not mean that at all; and it is a tragedy that it has been taken like that. It brings people into bondage. It says that their adornment is not to be just outward adornment but an inward thing. Phillips puts it beautifully: "The loveliness of an inner character." It does not mean that you are not to wear jewelry, nor have your hair done nicely ("elaborate coiffure", as Phillips puts it), but rather if you think that is adornment, you are mistaken. No one is going to tell me that Sarah didn't have a lot of jewelry, coming from Ur of the Chaldees, the creator of so much. That is not what it means. God may have dealings with us about these things and may say, "I want that away." Oh, very big things can depend upon our obedience to the Lord. It is the issue of His Lordship over us. However, let us be careful. We are saying that sisters should have within them this inner beauty, this gentleness of character, this readiness to fulfill their role. Then it goes on to the husbands and says that they ought "to be a stronger vessel giving honor to the weaker vessel that your prayers be not hindered." In other words, you can uncover yourself in your family relationships in such a way through disorder. The setting aside of divine order is one of the biggest problems we can face.

We have spoken mostly of individual believers getting uncovered, but the danger is just as real corporately. The root causes of corporate uncovering are basically the same as for the individual, especially certain things like the setting aside of divine order, the presumptuous claims, disobedience, and pride. These things can come to a whole company very easily. We have only to look at church history to see evidence for this on every page. Things that began so powerfully, so dynamically, ended up in absolute disarray. We have only to look around us on the present scene to see all the evidence we need. There are many groups that are divided or destroyed, although things started off so well with such great hope, with such a knowledge of the Lord and such an understanding of His way and will. I can go through one group after another, broken up, destroyed, paralyzed. What is it? It is this terrible question of uncovering.

But let me end on a more positive note. The Lord Jesus does ever live to make intercession. I think it was lovely what the Lord Jesus said in John 17:

Holy Father, keep them in thy name which thou hast given me, that they may be one, even as we are. While I was with them, I kept them in thy name which thou hast given me: and I guarded them, and not one of them perished, but the son of perdition; that the scripture might be fulfilled. John 17:11–12

The Lord Jesus often spent a night in prayer. Do you think it was covering them one by one? He heard so much; He heard the claims they made; He heard the conversation; He saw the collisions; He saw all these things we have listed. "I guarded them." Did He just guard them by word? Of course He did; but don't you think He guarded them in the secret place? They could not understand, and we get it so beautifully when they all said, "We will die with you, Lord." And He said, "Simon, Simon, Satan has obtained thee by request that he might sift thee as wheat. He has obtained you all. I have prayed for you, Simon, that your faith fail not." Don't you think there we have a picture, a foreshadowing, of our Lord's intercession in heaven? Don't you think as He sees us, He sees these ways in which we get ourselves uncovered, and He prays for each one of us by name before His Father's face? I can say that I have been preserved so far in spite of the many times that I have been uncovered. Surely, you can too. It is because He has said, "I have prayed for you that your faith fail not." Oh, may God help us! We have a wonderful Lord who has not only saved us but ever lives to make intercession.

Shall we pray?

Dear Lord, we cover now this time in Thy presence. We pray, Lord, that it will not just be negative but, in some way, Thou will make it positive. It is possible for us just to look upon all these dangers, all these ways of getting uncovered and become, perhaps, frightened in a wrong way, frightened of ever contributing, frightened of ever, in any way, sharing responsibility, frightened of ever going forward with Thy people. Oh Lord, we pray that Thou would preserve us from all such negative, in-turned thoughts. And grant, we pray, that we may look away to the One who is our covering and know what it is to be found in Him, not having a righteousness of our own but His own righteousness apart from the law—something Thou has provided. Oh Father, we pray that everyone of us might know what it is to abide in the Lord. So now, we commit ourselves to Thee in the name of our Lord, Jesus Christ. Amen.

5.
How to Come Back Under Covering

John 17:1–26

Lord, as we turn to this study we do so in faith. We thank Thee for those words, "life is given through Thy name"; and we are looking to Thee that everyone of us, in this time, may know just that—life given us through the name of our Lord Jesus Christ. We need life, Lord, more life, a fresh discovery of the power of Thy life. Oh beloved Lord, then meet us in this time. We abide by faith under the anointing that is on the Head, our Lord Jesus Christ. Grant, Lord, that we shall hear Thy voice and receive from Thee. We ask it in the name of our Lord Jesus. Amen.

We have looked at a number of things that are representative of very many other things by which we can get ourselves uncovered. I just want to underline one point here that we hardly touched. We have talked about the danger of the individual believer getting uncovered, but let us say with great emphasis that it is just as possible for companies of believers, churches and works to get uncovered. You may wonder how a whole company of believers could get uncovered, but it is quite possible. Sometimes, those inexplicable times of heaviness, darkness, insinuation, or shadow are because, unwittingly, there has been a corporate uncovering. Again, there are so many ways in which this can happen; but basically, it is the same as the ways in which an individual gets uncovered.

Not Loving One Another

It is perfectly possible, in a company, to get to such a pitch where there is no real love, where there is absolute division and an "againstness"; and the whole company is uncovered before God. Now it takes two to make division. You cannot be divided from someone who will not be divided. You withdraw, that is all; you are divisive. Where you have people absolutely up against each other, all taking sides, all fighting, all seeking to influence one another, then you get a corporate uncovering. I know of work after work which has floundered and broken, and believers who have simply broken up, on that one level.

Not Fearing the Lord

Oh, what a need there is in all these house meetings all over the country for a new awareness of the presence of the Lord. In the very places where there has been such an awareness of the presence of the Lord and such an experience of the presence of the Lord, there is all the danger of there not being any fear of the

Lord. I have been in some companies where people have almost put their feet up at the Lord's table. In one particular group, I was horrified to see people slovenly sitting around with their feet up. The idea was that this is a kind of house meeting, this is a home meeting; but there was no fear of the Lord. We would not dream of meeting royalty like that. We are here to remember what the Lord Jesus did for us. There was no lounging for Him when He sacrificed Himself for us on the cross. There was no sitting around with His feet up when He gave His body and blood for us. No fear of the Lord! Again and again, that kind of thing results in uncovering; and a whole work unwittingly gets waylaid by the enemy. Deception and delusion come in because there has first been uncovering through no fear of the Lord.

Making Presumptuous Claims

You can almost be certain that if a group or a company makes a presumptuous claim, they get uncovered. You know the kind–"We; we are it; we are something. Come to us; we have got it." Once that is corporately claimed, in that kind of way, there is an uncovering; and you can be almost certain the work will be knocked to pieces because of presumption. When God is at work, what can we do? We cannot deny that the Lord is at work among us. We cannot say that the Lord is not doing something, perhaps, singular or unique, because I know of such works. It is not good for the folks there to say, "It is not unique, it is not singular, this is quite normal", when it isn't. But it is the way it is said. It is different to give the glory to God and say, "We don't quite understand; we are the stupidest crowd in the world; but God is doing something among us and with us." But you can be perfectly sure that, before long, it will be knocked to pieces if people say: "We are something; come to us; we will tell you everything. If you want any instruction or help, we will put you right. We have got a great deliverance ministry here; bring anyone to us, we will deliver them all. Any work which claims such big things will be shot to pieces. "We are going into enemy territory; we are going to give it to the enemy." What happens? A few years afterwards, they have disappeared in the storm. You cannot find a trace of them. Presumptuous claims!

Not Heeding and Obeying the Anointing

It is perfectly possible to know that inner voice speaking to a company about a particular thing or another, warning that danger is there, and not to heed it. If that is not heeded, uncovering results corporately. We have learned this bitterly. On at least two occasions in our history, we have learned that we have been uncovered corporately. There was a warning voice or bell ringing in many of our spirits, but we were pushing it down and suppressing it, feeling that it was something else. We were making excuses not to heed and obey the anointing. It is better not to touch a thing if you have got doubt about it, better not to get involved with something if you have a question, than to go in with that inner alarm bell ringing; because you get uncovered. "As you are taught by Him, the anointing, so you abide in Him" (I John 2:27).

Being Disobedient

It is possible for a company to be disobedient! God is calling for a fresh step forward. God is calling for some new expression of His power and glory. A company teeters on the brink of it, wondering, "Should we, shouldn't we, should we, shouldn't we". And always there are those who say, "Oh no, there are reasons for not going forward." This is disobedience in a company. I think of works which are now nothing, absolutely nothing, where at one time, the glory of the Lord filled the whole company; where you knew that the Lord was powerfully and mightily present. Now it is gone and you can almost trace it to a point when God sought to take that company onward with Himself, and they refused and faltered.

Often, God speaks twice on the same thing. Isn't that interesting? I know of a particular work where, twenty years previously, a message came; twenty years later, the same message came, was rejected and the whole work floundered.

I think of another place (in Europe) where I once went to speak and I thought, as I was there, that I had never heard so much noise in all my life; and it wasn't a joyful noise either. The more I watched, the more I felt, inwardly, "There is something wrong here; this company has lost the way somewhere." And yet, I felt they had been on the way. I go into some works where I feel they have never been on the way corporately, but I felt this company had been on the way. After all this noise, they quieted down, finally, and I was asked to speak. As I spoke, I believe the Lord was there. Afterwards, the pastor, who did not speak a word of English, came up to me and said: "Brother,

I have had such a strange experience this evening. I have been listening to you and it has been as if you have disappeared and I have gone back to 1938 when we heard, almost word for word, this message." I had been speaking of Christ as our life corporately. Then I thought, "That sense I had in the time of prayer." But I just said to the brother, "Well, I am very interested."

"It was a high water mark. It was simply tremendous. You would not know him because he was Chinese. He only had one night in the capital city and he came here. You would not know him because he is not a known man."

"Really? It wasn't Watchman Nee, was it?" (He couldn't speak English and, at that time, The Normal Christian Life was not in this particular language. It was only in English.)

His mouth dropped open, "Why, good gracious me! Yes, he came with a certain missionary here."

That was the explanation. All those years later, God sent me back with the same message and I didn't even know the history. God never judges a work or a company before He speaks to it at least twice. That work is nothing today. That was about seven or eight years ago. It is absolutely nothing! God speaks to us, "See that you don't harden your heart."

Today, oh that ye would hear his voice! Harden not your heart as at Meribah. Psalm 95:7b–8a

Setting Aside Divine Order

It is so easy to set aside divine order and override someone, where they have been placed in the body, or someone's ministry or function, as if it is not there. In this way we uncover ourselves. I remember some years ago, a particular sister walked into this place with another sister when no one was here. They saw a mirror hanging on the wall and they thought to themselves, "That mirror should not be there." They took it down and put it up over the Lord's treasury and took down a picture over the Lord's treasury and put it up over the chair. They left a little notice which simply said, "By order of Mrs. so-and-so." It was, of course, a declaration of war. We didn't do anything at all. We just left it exactly as it was while we prayed about it and heard from the Lord: "You shall reverse it." Together, we reversed it. That sister died some years later, but it was the beginning of uncovering. You cannot do those kinds of things and get away with it—not on church ground. You may get away with murder in a congregation, but you will not get away with it if there is any expression of the church at all, because you come face to face with the living God and with divine order and government. The people may be weak; they may appear fragile and frail; they may act stupid and dim; but the fact is, it is divine order, and we have to be very careful of divine order.

We have only to look around today to see the tragic evidence of this uncovering in so many companies and groups of believers that began in the right way and, somehow or other, now have completely floundered. "Wherefore let him that thinketh he standeth take heed lest he fall" (1 Corinthian 10:12). "Let them that think they stand take heed, lest they fall."

The Intercession of the Lord Jesus

When we begin to see the many ways in which we can get uncovered, how real the danger is and just how much evidence there is of it on all sides, the intercession of the Lord Jesus becomes really precious and wonderful. I do not suppose anyone who thinks he stands feels any need of the intercession of the Lord Jesus; but once you begin to realize the dangers that lurk and just what the enemy's devices and designs are, the intercession of the Lord Jesus becomes wonderfully precious. I am here today because of the intercession of the Lord Jesus. You may not know it, but you are too. He, more than any other, sees the danger, knows our fragility, our frailty and our weakness, and prays for us. We know that the Lord Jesus does not spend all His intercession at the right hand of the Father praying for us as individuals or that we might be covered. We know that. We know that the intercessory ministry of the Lord Jesus reaches right back before times eternal and on to the ages to come. He is praying for the fulfillment of the purpose of God. He is praying for the preparation of the bride. He is waiting, reminding the Father that His work is finished, that His triumph is complete until every enemy has been made the footstool of His feet. We know that the intercessory ministry of the Lord Jesus is far bigger and far more comprehensive than just praying for our covering. But He did pray for Peter personally, and how lovely that was: "Satan has desired or obtained you by request" (See Luke 22:31). In the Greek, it is plural–"you all"–and that is how the New English Bible and Phillips says it. "Satan has obtained you all, all eleven of you, by request." Then He turned to Peter and said: "I have prayed for thee (singular) that your faith fail not." It is quite clear to me that the Lord Jesus prayed for everyone of the eleven. But what a wonderful word the Lord Jesus gave to Peter, the leader of the twelve, who was to be the one who fell so terribly, who fell the most devastatingly: "But I have prayed for thee."

Who shall lay anything to the charge of God's elect? It is God that justifieth; who is he that condemneth? It is Christ Jesus that died, yea rather, that was raised from the dead, who is at the right hand of God, who also maketh intercession for us. Romans 8:33–34

Wherefore also he is able to save to the uttermost them that draw near unto God through him, seeing he ever liveth to make intercession for them. Hebrews 7:25

The emphasis here is on "to the uttermost". However terrible the circumstances, however complex the background, however difficult the temperament or constitution of the person, He can save to the uttermost seeing He ever liveth to make intercession". He got Mary Magdalene out of all that background of evil that was in the woman. He got it out of others. If God can do this in the first century, can't He do it in the twentieth? Is the twentieth century more than the first for God? Is God's power less able?

But he, because he abideth for ever, hath his priesthood unchangeable. Hebrews 7:24

The priesthood of our Lord Jesus Christ that was able to get these folks in the first century through is exactly the same today. "He ever lives to make intercession for them." "Who shall lay anything to the charge of God's elect?" "Who is he that condemneth or accuseth?" "Christ maketh intercession for us." "Who shall separate us from the love of Christ?"

> For Christ entered not into a holy place made with hands, like in pattern to the true; but into heaven itself, now to appear before the face of God for us. Hebrews 9:24

Isn't that little phrase "for us" wonderful? He appears before the face of God for us. Let it sink into you. Before we can ever talk about how to get recovered when we have become uncovered, we have to understand what the Lord Jesus is doing and understand what lies behind all this.

> Having then a great high priest, who hath passed through the heavens, Jesus the Son of God, let us hold fast our confession. For we have not a high priest that cannot be touched with the feeling of our infirmities; but one that hath been in all points tempted like as we are, yet without sin. Let us therefore draw near with boldness unto the throne of grace, that we may receive mercy, and may find grace to help us in time of need. Hebrews 4:14–16

Why does it say, "... that we may receive mercy"? Is it not the fact that, somehow or other, in all our frailty and weakness, we have become ourselves uncovered? Don't stay away from the throne of grace because of that. Go before the throne of grace that you may receive mercy and grace to help in time of need: mercy to cover the failure and grace to get through. That is the intercessory ministry of our Lord Jesus Christ who is touched with the feeling of our infirmities. "Peter, I prayed for you." It is as if Peter's own heart beat in the heart of the Lord Jesus; as if He knew from the inside the frailty and weakness of His dear disciple, Peter; as if, somehow, He knew the inside, the depth of which he was capable; as if He knew how he walked on a tightrope. He was touched with the feeling of his infirmities. He knew what was in Peter. He knows what is in you. He knows from the inside. The Lord Jesus isn't just up there; He is in us. He sees us from the inside. He understands the inner workings of our minds, our imaginations, our conceptions and the motive forces that govern us. "He is touched with the feeling of our infirmities"—not judging, but interceding.

"Peter, I prayed for you." Wouldn't it have been easy for the Lord to say to Peter: "You are a hopeless, empty tin can. You are just a windbag, full of big words; and in My hour of need, you are going to let Me down. What kind of disciple are you? You are just a ratbag. The sooner you know it, the better; then when you have discovered it, perhaps you will get converted and I will receive you back."

No, not a single word! The Lord was absolutely true. "Simon, Simon, Satan hath obtained thee by asking that he may sift thee as wheat, but I have prayed for thee that thy faith fail not." What faith? The faith is not in Peter; the faith is in the Son of God. The Lord has absolute faith concerning Peter that he is going to come through. He has prayed for him. The Lord Jesus can say this of you and me as He looks at us: "Oh, you don't understand how the enemy wants you, how he seeks like a roaring lion whom he may devour, but I have prayed for you. I know you. I know your circumstances, and I know the complexity of your nature. I love you."

There is something absolutely wonderful here for "Jesus Christ is the same yesterday, today and forever." The Jesus who said yesterday, "I prayed for you, Peter, that your faith fail not" is the same Lord Jesus today. He knows us so well. He knows our corporate aspirations and longing of our hearts. He knows where we want to go and what we want to do.

Kept in the Name

In the high priestly prayer of the Lord Jesus Christ in John 17, we see the most blessed intimation of this intercessory ministry of the Lord Jesus concerning covering.

> *I manifested thy name unto the men whom thou gavest me out of the world. John 17:6*

What a wonderful phrase: "I manifested thy name". Now we all know that this title or this term "the name of the Lord" means covering. There is no meaning of authority; it means covering.

> *The name of the Lord is a strong tower; The righteous runneth into it, and is safe. Proverbs 18:10*

Holy Father, keep them in thy name which
thou has given me. John 17:11

What is that Name? Jesus. What does it mean to be kept in the Name? It means kept in all that the Name stands for; kept in the Person of the Lord Jesus; kept abiding in Him; kept hidden in Him; kept where God has put us, "in the Lord Jesus".

While I was with them I kept them in thy name. John 17:12a

If the Lord Jesus could keep those eleven hopeless disciples without the Holy Spirit in them, don't you think you are a subject for His keeping power? Don't you think He can keep you? I suppose those eleven were just like us. Sometimes, we can even take a superior position about them and feel they are worse than us. We might even think, "If we had been with the Lord for those three years, surely we wouldn't be acting like that." After three years of their failure and inability to reach that level of understanding and revelation, He said, "I kept them in thy name. Here I am at the end of three years and I have still got them, except the son of perdition, the only one who was lost. The other eleven I have kept in thy name." He covered them. What was He doing when He prayed those nights, if He was not also praying for their covering? He kept them in His name. "I guarded them and not one of them perished" (John 17:12b).

I pray not that thou shouldest take them from the world, but
that thou shouldest keep them from the evil one. John 17:15

"Lead us not into temptation but deliver us from the evil one." This is the prayer the Lord Jesus taught us to pray; it is the pattern prayer. We have an intimation of the kind of prayer that the Lord Jesus is praying for us now. We see it in John:

> Neither for these only do I pray, but for them also
> that believe on me through their word. John 17:20

That is you and me. So we know that our Lord Jesus, at the right hand of God, the Father, is praying like this: "I manifested my name to them. Holy Father, keep them in Thy name which Thou has given me."

> And I made known unto them thy name, and will
> make it known; that the love wherewith thou lovedst
> me may be in them, and I in them. John 17:26

It was not only all that He had given to them, but He was going to make it known through the Spirit. He was thinking, of course, of the Acts when, for the first time, these dear old disciples, so dim and failing, suddenly saw what the Name of the Lord meant. They went everywhere, doing all things in the Name of the Lord Jesus. They turned the world upside down by the Name of the Lord Jesus. They knew it meant both covering and authority. He prays today: "I guard them. Not one of them shall perish."

Unity

There is one other point we ought to look at in this prayer, and it is the question of unity—our unity with the Father and with the Son, and our unity with one another.

> *And I am no more in the world, and these are in the world, and I come to thee. Holy Father, keep them in thy name which thou hast given me, that they may be one, even as we are. John 17:11*

> *That they may all be one; even as thou, Father, art in me, and I in thee, that they also may be in us: that the world may believe that thou didst send me. And the glory which thou hast given me I have given unto them; that they may be one, even as we are one; I in them, and thou in me, that they may be perfected into one; that the world may know that thou didst send me, and lovedst them, even as thou lovedst me. John 17:21–23*

The prayer of the Lord Jesus is over this question of keeping us abiding in reality in the Father and in the Son, by the Spirit, and therefore, in unity with one another. Anything that divides, anything that destroys that unity, anything that injures the Name of the Lord Jesus Christ is a plague and it will cause uncovering. So the Lord Jesus prays that we may be one; that we may be kept in that unity and that it may be exactly the same as the unity between the Father and the Son; and that we may be kept together in the bundle of life. How serious it is!

For this cause many among you are weak and
sickly, and not a few sleep. 1 Corinthians 11:30

They have eaten judgment to themselves by not discerning the Lord's body. The Lord's body is not just a physical thing. The Lord's body is that great spiritual, eternal reality of which you and I, by the grace of God, are part. We have been joined to the Lord in one Spirit. Therefore, because we are one with Him, we are one with one another. So the easiest way for the enemy to get us uncovered is to destroy that unity; and the Lord Jesus Christ prays for that unity. If that is so, what intercession the Lord Jesus must be engaged in to keep us in the unity of the Spirit!

The basis for such intercession is unshakably sure. In the offering of Himself once for all, Christ has made provision for every single one of us to be covered, to stay covered, and to get recovered when we become uncovered. Now let me just say that again. The basis for this intercessory ministry of the Lord Jesus is absolutely unshakeable and sure. What is it? Does it depend on your zeal? Does it depend on your devotion? No, it is founded upon His own finished work and what He has done in the offering of Himself once for all. In the sacrifice of Himself once for all time, He has made provision that every single one of us, from the dimmest child of God in the whole world to the most spiritually intelligent, from the youngest to the oldest in the Lord, might stay covered, and if anything should happen, get back under covering.

Being Presented Before God Without Spot

But he, when he had offered one sacrifice for sins
forever, sat down on the right hand of God; henceforth
expecting till his enemies be made the footstool of his
feet. For by one offering he hath perfected for ever
them that are sanctified. Hebrews 10:12–14

All the provision is there, not only for our salvation, but for our sanctification and for our being presented before God without spot.

Wherefore also he is able to save to the uttermost them that
draw near unto God through him, seeing he ever liveth to
make intercession for them. For such a high priest became
us, holy, guileless, undefiled, separated from sinners, and
made higher than the heavens; who needeth not daily, like
those high priests, to offer up sacrifices, first for his own
sins, and then for the sins of the people: for this he did once
for all, when he offered up himself. Hebrews 7:25–27

The basis of this intercession is that He has offered up Himself
once for all. In one of the first studies in this series on covering,
we spoke of the five-fold offering of our Lord Jesus Christ as
we find it in Leviticus in the first seven chapters. We find that
in the old economy, there was a five-fold offering: the burnt
offering, the meal offering, the peace offering, the sin offering,
and the trespass offering. Every single part of the believer's
life was covered by that five-fold offering, whether it was

*worship and service, humanity, fellowship and communion,
or sin wittingly committed or unwittingly committed. Every
single part was covered by the sacrifice of the Lord Jesus
Christ. "The Lord Jesus would keep us from falling" Jude 24*

*Now to Him Who is able to keep you without stumbling,
or slipping, or falling and to present (you) unblemished
(blameless and faultless) before the presence of His glory—with
unspeakable, ecstatic delight—in triumphant joy and exultation,
To the one only God, our Savior through Jesus Christ our
Lord, be glory (splendor), majesty, might, and dominion, and
power and authority, before all time and now and forever—
unto all the ages of eternity. Amen. Jude 24 Amplified*

The Lord Jesus is able to present us before His Father's face
with ecstatic delight; and even the Lord Jesus, Himself, will
be speechless because He has got us there. If He is speechless,
we should be. We shall stand there dumbfounded—just the very
thought that, finally, He has got us there, faultless, without
spot or blemish. How can the Lord Jesus get you and me there
without spot or blemish? Do we not all have spots and blemishes?
The only way He can do it is through the sacrifice of Himself
once for all. He has not only saved us to the uttermost but He has
sanctified us. Oh, that we would go in by the Spirit and possess
what is ours; that we would take what is ours that He might have
that ecstatic, unspeakable joy of finally bringing us before His
Father's face. I find so wonderful the very thought of how the Lord
could get such a vile creature as I—so difficult, so rebellious and
such unlikely material—into His Father's presence and present

me. Why should He present you or me? Are we so presentable? We would shrivel up in the presence of His Father were the glory of God to appear before us; but not through His sacrifice. There is covering and provision that we may be changed into the same image from glory to glory.

Finishing The Course

The Apostle Paul had many faults. There are some people who think that the Apostle Paul had no failings or faults; but I think that in the book of Acts, when you take your rose-colored spectacles off, you see that he is there, warts and all. It is not one of those beautifully touched-up photographs. The Apostle Paul is there; and when you read his letters, he is simply marvelous. He is so much himself that he gives the game away every time. Again and again, we find him saying, "Now you have pushed me into boasting. I shouldn't have done it."

We would say: "Now a godly person would not write like that. Cut all that out. You cannot talk like that." He is talking about having such a bad time because he had written a letter rebuking them. Then he spent sleepless nights because he thought he had done the wrong thing, until he got back a letter saying it had humbled the whole lot of them. Then he was glad. Little did he know that it was all Scripture. If the dear old apostle had known that it was all Scripture and was going to be read by countless saints down through the ages, he would have become so self-conscious and cut out half of what he had written. "Cut that out, cut that out. We cannot have them all talking and reading that kind of thing; it is too private." He put himself on the page.

Nevertheless, we find him saying in II Timothy 4:7, "I have finished the course." It is the grace of God for any man like that to be able to say,

"I have finished the course; I have not gone off the course." Oh, the believers we know who have gone off the course! But haven't we all gone off and had to be put back? The apostle could say at the end, "I have finished the course; I am exactly where I should have been, by the grace of God." He did not say, "This is the great Apostle Paul; I have done all this." Oh, no! He said, "I have kept the faith, I have finished the course, I have fought the fight: henceforth..." What a wonderful position to get to. In the previous letter, he said he was the chief of all sinners. Now if the chief of all sinners can finish the course, what about you and me? The apostle had his faith truly focused and centered in the Lord Jesus Christ, Himself, as the One who not only offered up Himself for him but was interceding for him. He was keeping him on course like one of those wonderful compasses that immediately tell the slightest degree of moving away. Only the Lord Jesus can keep us absolutely on course.

We have two unshakably sure things: the finished work of Christ through which we can be saved to the uttermost, and the Lord Jesus Christ as intercessor, mediator and advocate.

My little children, these things write I unto you that ye may not sin. And if any man sin, we have an Advocate with the Father, Jesus Christ the righteous: and he is the propitiation for our sins; and not for ours only, but also for the whole world. 1 John 2:1–2

He is both Advocate and Sacrifice. We have these two unshakably sure things. How wonderful that is! No wonder the Apostle Paul said:

> Who shall separate us from the love of Christ? For I am persuaded, that neither death, nor life, nor angels, nor principalities, nor things present, nor things to come, nor powers, nor height, nor depth, nor any other creature, shall be able to separate us from the love of God, which is in Christ Jesus our Lord. Romans 8:38–39

It is in Him. While we are there, nothing can separate us. We are in the place of absolute safety.

How to Get Back Under Covering

Nevertheless, although there is no need for us to get uncovered, and indeed, every encouragement not to, the sad fact is that most of us do get uncovered, sometime or other, and so do most companies of God's children. What should we do when we know we have become uncovered? We must learn to take immediate action; and when I say immediate action, I mean it! The moment you become aware that you have become uncovered, take immediate action. Don't leave such a condition for minutes, let alone days. You have no idea the danger you are in while you are uncovered, because it only takes Satan a minute to deceive.

For many of us, our salvation took place in a minute. Suddenly light dawned, suddenly we saw, suddenly the things of God lived to us. One moment we were dead, the next moment we were alive.

Spiritual things are like that. When you have become uncovered, don't leave it. However, we should not get into an introspective state and say, "Oh dear, dear, I am sure I have left it for weeks and weeks and months." But listen; get this clear: when you become aware you are uncovered, the Holy Spirit is the most wonderful Person. He is not the accuser, as many believers think. He is the Advocate within; He is the One who comes alongside, the Paraclete, the Counselor, the Comforter. The moment He knows that you are uncovered, you will hear that gracious voice of the Spirit of God just saying, "Get back, get back." He never says, "You are uncovered!" He says, "Get back, get back; something has gone wrong." The ministry of the Holy Spirit is so gracious. As soon as you know you are uncovered, don't say, "I will go see brother so-and-so tonight;" or "I will have a time of prayer tonight;" or "I will be seeing so-and-so next week, I will do it then." No! Don't leave it. Once the Holy Spirit is speaking to your heart about this matter, take immediate action. Get under covering straight away. There are four basic things that we will consider here so you will always know what to do.

Recognize That You Are Uncovered

This may seem so utterly simple, but many people have a terrible battle over this. Oh, the excuses people make! They say, "Well, you know I was pushed into it;" or "It is my circumstances." They will not just simply say, "I have become uncovered." We all get uncovered. We don't mean to, we are encouraged not to, but the sad fact is we do. You must recognize the fact that you are uncovered. The need is for absolute and strict honesty with yourself. If you do not have this strict honesty with yourself, you cannot get back under covering.

I can think of case after case over the years where something happened, and people just could not recognize it; they just could not say, "I got uncovered on that point." I think of a sister who died. When she was so ill, she asked me and some of the other brothers to come and lay hands on her. We went in fear and trembling. We knew that to lay hands on that sister in that condition would work the opposite way and would bring death and not life, but what could we do? We went, having prayed much about it beforehand. We said to her, "Have you anything to confess?" And she looked straight at us and said, "Nothing at all." Then we knew that the sentence was confirmed. We laid hands on her, and I think it was a week or so later she passed away. Every time we prayed for that dear sister, a new attack came.

We must recognize uncovering. When you think of it, it is so simple to say: "I have become uncovered. I said something I should not have said. I did something I should not have done." It is as simple as that. "Walk in the light as God is in the light." Don't reduce it to grayness, to twilight, to the in-between or dusk. Don't just put out a great smoke screen of excuses: "I was pushed into it. So-and-so was saying so-and-so to me and so-and-so poured this story into my ear, and I was pushed into it." You can make excuse after excuse, but the fact is you have become uncovered. Don't make excuses. Recognize the fact.

"Walk in the light as God is in the light." What does that mean? Just come out into the light. When you come out into the light, you see things as they really are. When you are groping around in the dark, you cannot see things as they are; but when you come out into the light, you see things as they really are. Suddenly you see. If you go into a dark room that you don't know, you grope around, finding out what that is, and then there is something else, and so on. You put on the light and suddenly you see there is a table there and a chair there and a plant stand there and so on. You see it when the light is on. "Walk in the light as God is in the light."

Also, in this matter of recognizing that you are uncovered, you need to confess clearly and concisely. If you have said something, retract the very words that you said. Don't try to make out that you did not say it. Simply retract the very words that you used. If you have taken a position against someone, retract. That is repentance. Some people think that repentance is only for those who are not saved. It isn't. When we get into trouble, we have to repent. Otherwise, we will get back into the same trouble again and again and again. We have to see it for what it is and call it by its name. I have done so-and-so. Please forgive me. I have been stupid." The Holy Spirit, our Advocate within, will give us the understanding and the help we need in this matter. Some may say: "Well, I am not quite sure. I know I have become uncovered, but I do not know how." You ask the Holy Spirit. Without accusing you, He will bring to your memory the exact point at which uncovering came. The Holy Spirit is the One who guards us. His job is to keep us covered. His whole job is to keep us in Christ and abiding in Christ. Now the Holy Spirit knows exactly where uncovering came in, and He will give you His help and understanding, if you will only be honest. We have a spirit in us, and the Holy Spirit is in our spirit. He will just say to you, "It was so-and- so", and it will click. When it happens, you say:

"That is it! I knew it, that is it!" When you have had an experience like that, you know it. Something inside you says: "Ah, how stupid of me. Of course that is it." Your whole being is flooded with light. You are back and you know it.

By Faith Retake Your Divinely Given Position in Christ

First, recognize that you are uncovered. Second, by faith, retake your divinely given position in Christ. Don't just confess and say, "Well, now that is all done." Say, "Lord, I take my position again in Thy Son; I take my place in Him." No matter what the accuser roars (as it says in one of our hymns), however much he says your case is hopeless and God will not hear you or listen to you, by faith, retake the place which is yours through the finished work of Christ and the grace of God. Remember, that place in God's Son was given you through His finished work, not because of anything in you. God didn't say: "Well, you know I rather like so-and-so. So-and-so is rather sweet and decent, so I think I should extend My saving grace to so-and-so."

He did not save you on that basis. He saved you as a worthless rebel, bankrupt.

You cannot retake that position by saying: "Now Lord, I am all polished up. You know I am really something. I will go out house to house on Wednesdays; I will go out witnessing on Sunday; and I will spend an hour or two in prayer. I will join that intercessor's business. What else can I do, Lord? Of course, if you really want me I will offer myself for service somewhere. I will go cleaning on Friday evenings as well. I never did like that. I may even do stewarding, Lord." All those things may be right, but do not think for a single moment that is the basis for taking your position again in the Lord Jesus. If you make that the basis, you are on the basis of works, and then you will have an evil conscience. All the time, Satan will come and say you are not doing good enough. He will drive you and you will think it is the Lord who is driving you. You are not up to scratch. That is not your basis. Your basis is the Lord Jesus died for you; your basis is that He laid down His life for you; your basis is that He sacrificed Himself. When you come, you say: "Father, I am uncovered. Forgive me, Lord. Here is the reason. This is what I did, Lord. Forgive me. Cleanse me. Now, by faith, I take my place in Your Son again, through Your grace, through His blood and through His finished work.

I hide myself, Father in Him." You are back again to use the name of the Lord.

Put Right Whatever Is Wrong No Matter What the Cost

This is where most people stumble. Sometimes, this is very costly to our pride, especially when it involves others or the whole church; but there is no back door to covering. There is an if. "If we walk in the light as God is in the light, we have fellowship one with another and the blood of Jesus Christ, God's Son, cleanses us from all sin." We have got to walk in the light.

Sometimes, this involves us in putting something right. Some people say: "But is that really necessary? After all, the finished work of Jesus Christ has dealt with it." You will never learn your lesson until you are prepared to humble yourself. If you have said something or done something–maybe one of these ways we have talked about in which we get uncovered–you will never learn your lesson if you only say, "I put it right with the Lord." Sooner or later, you will fall again on the same thing because it has not been put right. You have got to go and say to whoever it is, "I am very sorry." "Lord, give me grace. I will go. I will just put this right." When you have done that, it is hard, but it is burnt into you. Something is written indelibly in your spirit. You think twice again before you ever go through that experience. "Oh, I could not bear to do that again and have to go to someone else."

It is just like little children. I know there is not much discipline these days, but this is how we were taught when we were young. We were taught that if we did so-and-so we would have to do so-and-so. If we had good parents, they stuck to it and we had to do it. Oh, the agonies we used to go through as kids. I remember I wrote a letter to a particular person down the road about their son, whom I disliked very much. My father said I had to go and actually apologize. I went through agonies. I found out years afterward that family thought it terribly funny. He was Dutch and I felt all the severity of the way he looked at me when he opened the door. I went in trembling, and he took me into his study, which didn't help. After listening to it all, he said, "You know this kind of thing causes wars." But I never wrote a letter like that again in my life. It was not that I wasn't tempted to write a letter. Two or three times, I could have sat down with great ease and written the same kind of letter; but I could not go through all that again. Oh, the humiliation of it, and the being broken down with it all. No! That is how we learn it does not pay. So put right whatever is wrong. Remember, there is no back door to covering.

Learn the Lesson

When we have become uncovered, there is always a cause. No one slides into it. It does not just happen. We are absolutely safe in Christ, unless we have become uncovered. So we must learn the lesson. What is the cause? Some people are all the time realizing: "Oh, this has happened. Now Lord, just forgive me and cleanse me." Then the same thing happens again and again and again because they will not learn the lesson.

The Bible has some very harsh words to say about fools. A fool is someone who will not receive instruction. A fool is not someone who makes a mistake, but one who makes the same mistake again and again and again. That is what the Bible says. Now the basis of that folly is the inability to learn, or if you like, an unteachable spirit. "I am not going to listen to that; I know it anyway." But you don't. You cannot teach anyone unless they are ready to say, "Yes, I am wrong there; how should I have done it?" Learn the lesson. It is much better to learn to stay covered at all times than to have to continually get back under covering. "Why have I become uncovered? Let me learn the lesson. I will not do it again." That is the way of progress.

Those who refuse either to recognize that they have become uncovered or to learn the lesson, invariably go off course. I can say that quite dogmatically. They invariably go off course because they will not recognize the point of departure; so they are off without any possibility of the Lord bringing them back. A deviation has started.

We want to be those who have learned how to stay in Christ at all times and to abide in Him. When we have become uncovered, we want to be those who have learned that we must take immediate action not to stay in the condition of tremendous danger one moment longer than our having become aware of it.

Everything is in Christ–all the fulness, all the provision, all the treasures of wisdom and knowledge, all the grace and all the power. He is fortress, stronghold, strong tower, rock of defense, refuge, temple, sanctuary, covert and hiding place.

Oh, that we could learn what it is to stay in the place where God has put us, where we are absolutely safe. May God teach us this simple lesson.

1. Recognize you are uncovered.
2. Retake your position by faith in Christ.
3. Put right whatever is wrong, whatever the cost.
4. Learn the lesson.

Shall we pray:

Now Lord, we pray that Thou would indeed teach us this lesson. Write it on our hearts. All of us, in one way or another, need this message. We need to know how to take immediate action. Oh, write it, Lord, in practical terms in every one of our lives. Where there is any uncovering, we pray that we might know what to do; and may everyone of us who is covered learn how to stay covered. May we know what it is to have our life hid with Christ in Thee. We ask it in the name of our Lord Jesus. Amen.

6.
Examples of Covering in the Old Testament

Numbers 16:1–38

Now Korah son of Izhar, son of Kohath, son of Levi, with the Reubenites Dathan and Abiram sons of Eliab, and On son of Peleth, challenged the authority of Moses. With them in their revolt were two hundred and fifty Israelites, all men of rank in the community, conveners of assembly and men of good standing. They confronted Moses and Aaron and said to them, `You take too much upon yourselves. Every member of the community is holy and the Lord is among them all. Why do you set yourselves up above the assembly of the Lord?'

When Moses heard this, he prostrated himself, and he said to Korah and all his company, `Tomorrow morning the Lord shall declare who is his, who is holy and may present offerings to him. The man whom the Lord chooses shall present them. This is what you must do, you, Korah, and all your company: you must take censers and put fire in them, and then place incense on them before the Lord tomorrow.

The man whom the Lord then chooses is the man who is holy. You take too much upon yourselves, you sons of Levi.' Moses said to Korah, 'Now listen, you sons of Levi. Is it not enough for you that the God of Israel has set you apart from the community of Israel, bringing you near him to maintain the service of the Tabernacle of the Lord and to stand before the community as their ministers? He has brought you near him and your brother Levites with you; now you seek the priesthood as well. That is why you and all your company have combined together against the Lord. What is Aaron that you should make these complaints against him?'

Moses sent to fetch Dathan and Abiram sons of Eliab, but they answered, 'We are not coming. Is it a small thing that you have brought us away from a land flowing with milk and honey to let us die in the wilderness? Must you also set yourself up as prince over us? What is more, you have not brought us unto a land flowing with milk and honey, nor have you given us fields and vineyards to inherit. Do you think you can hoodwink men like us? We are not coming.' This answer made Moses very angry, and he said to the Lord, 'Take no notice of their murmuring. I have not taken from them so much as a single ass; I have done no wrong to any of them.'

Moses said to Korah, 'Present yourselves before the Lord tomorrow you and all your company, you and they and Aaron. Each man of you is to take his censer and put incense on it. Then you shall present them before the Lord with their two hundred and fifty censers, and you and Aaron shall also bring your censers.' So each man took his censer and put fire in it and placed incense on it; Moses and Aaron took their stand at the entrance to the Tent of the Presence, and Korah gathered his whole company together and faced them at the entrance to the Tent of the Presence.

Then the glory of the Lord appeared to the whole community. And the Lord spoke to Moses and Aaron and said, 'Stand apart from this company, so that I may make an end of them in a single instant.' But they prostrated themselves and said, 'O God, God of the spirits of all mankind, if one man sins, wilt thou be angry with the whole community?' But the Lord said to Moses, 'Tell them to stand back from the dwellings of Korah, Dathan and Abiram.' So Moses rose and went to Dathan and Abiram, and the elders of Israel followed him. He said to the whole community, 'Stand well away from the tents of these wicked men; touch nothing of theirs, or you will be swept away because of all their sins.' So they moved away from the places occupied by Korah, Dathan and Abiram. Now Dathan and Abiram, holding themselves erect, had come out to the entrance of their tents with their wives, their sons, and their dependents. Then Moses said, 'This shall prove to you that it is the Lord who sent me to do all these things, and it was not my own heart that prompted me. If these men die a natural death and share the common fate of man, then the Lord has not sent me; but if the Lord makes a great chasm, and the ground opens its mouth and swallows them and all that is theirs, and they go down alive to Sheol, then you will know that these men have held the Lord in contempt.'

Hardly had Moses spoken when the ground beneath them split: the earth opened its mouth and swallowed them and their homes—all the followers of Korah and all their property. They went down alive into Sheol with all that they had; the earth closed over them, and they vanished from the assembly. At their cries all the Israelites round them fled, shouting, 'Look to yourselves! the earth will swallow us up.' Meanwhile fire had come out from the Lord and burnt up the two hundred and fifty men who were presenting the incense.

Then the Lord spoke to Moses and said, 'Bid Eleazar son of Aaron the priest set aside the censers from the burnt remains, and scatter the fire from them far and wide, because they are holy. And the censers of these men who sinned at the cost of their lives you shall make into beaten plates to cover the altar; they are holy, because they have been presented before the Lord. Let them be a sign to the Israelites.' (New English Bible)

Numbers 16:41–50

Next day all the community of the Israelites raised complaints against Moses and Aaron and taxed them with causing the death of some of the Lord's people. As they gathered against Moses and Aaron, they turned towards the Tent of the Presence and saw that the cloud covered it, and the glory of the Lord appeared. Moses and Aaron came to the front of the Tent of the Presence, and the Lord spoke to Moses and Aaron and said, 'Stand well clear of this community, so that in a single instant I may make an end of them.' Then they prostrated *themselves, and Moses said to Aaron, 'Take your censer, put fire from the altar in it, set incense on it, and go with it quickly to the assembled community to make atonement for them. Wrath has gone forth already from the presence of the Lord. The plague has begun.' So Aaron took his censer, as Moses had said, ran into the midst of the assembly and found that the plague had begun among the people. He put incense on the censer and made atonement for the people, standing between the dead and the living, and the plague stopped. Fourteen thousand seven hundred died of it, in addition to those who had died for the offence of Korah. When Aaron came back to Moses at the entrance to the Tent of the Presence, the plague had stopped. (New English Bible)*

Shall we pray?

Oh Lord, we are dependent on Thee for speaking and hearing alike. Lord, draw near, we pray, and make real to us Thy word by Thy Holy Spirit. Instruct us. We ask it in the name of our Lord Jesus. Amen.

We know that all things recorded in the Old Testament were recorded for our instruction.

Now these things happened unto them by way of example; and they were written for our admonition, upon whom the ends of the ages are come. Wherefore let him that thinketh he standeth take heed lest he fall. 1 Corinthians 10:11–12

We have often heard that word, "Wherefore let him that thinketh he standeth take heed lest he fall"; but, in this context, it is said of examples recorded in the Old Testament for our admonition and instruction. So the story we have read, along with the others, are meant to be examples or illustrations for our instruction and education. This matter of covering is illustrated everywhere in the Old Testament and all I can do is select some of the more obvious examples, beginning in the first book of the Bible, Genesis.

Adam and Eve

And the Lord God made for Adam and for his wife coats of skins, and clothed them. Genesis 3:21

And the eyes of them both were opened, and they knew that they were naked; and they sewed fig-leaves together, and made themselves aprons. Genesis 3:7

And in process of time it came to pass, that Cain brought of the fruit of the ground an offering unto the Lord. And Abel, he also brought of the firstlings of his flock and of the fat thereof. And the Lord had respect unto Abel and to his offering: but unto Cain and to his offering he had not respect. And Cain was very wroth and his countenance fell. Genesis 4:3–5

Here we have the first example illustrating this whole matter of covering. God covered Adam and Eve when they fell into sin, at the cost of blood. The only way He could clothe them with skins was by the death or sacrifice of another life. There is a vast difference between being covered with the skins God provided for Adam and Eve and taking leaves and sewing them together. There was no sacrifice there; there was no pain there; there was no death there; there was no blood shed there. God sacrificed a life and shed blood in order to cover them. The old rabbis tell us that it was a lamb that was sacrificed. Although it is not mentioned here, I should imagine that it was, in fact, a lamb. In the story we read in chapter four, Abel took a one year old lamb from his flock, just like the Passover lamb, sacrificed it and God had respect. In other words, Adam and Eve had obviously passed on to their sons the fact that the only way to be covered in the presence of God was by the sacrifice of another life. Cain, by bringing the fruit of the ground, tried to perpetuate the mistake that Adam and Eve made in clothing themselves with leaves. So right at the beginning of the Bible, immediately after sin entered into the human race, immediately after man and woman fell, God gave us the Lamb as our salvation and as our acceptance with Him. We are covered by the Lamb.

One of the greatest problems with believers is the fig leaves they are always sewing together. It is incredible how most of us who relegate this subject of justification to the spiritual kindergarten are suffering from our weakness of understanding over it. Therefore, we try to rake up dead works to please God all the time. We try to produce fruit from the ground—the work of our hands—that will make Him pleased. It is something that has not gone through the death and resurrection of Calvary, that process of the cross. We are trying to bring something else to God and win His favor. We try to get His acceptance and somehow make Him feel, "Well, he is a good chap; she is a good girl; marvelous, really." Unwittingly, that becomes the foundation or the basis of our acceptance before God.

The leaves that we gather to sew together as garments so we can come before God are pretty and, oftentimes, quite long lasting; but all the time God has no respect for it at all. You may be the sweetest person, the most honest person, the most hard-working person, the most upright person; but if you come in the leaves, God has no respect for it at all. If you bring the fruit of the ground, He has no respect at all. You may be rotten, but if you bring the Lamb, God immediately accepts it. It is the Lamb that matters; and that is simply what covering is, as far as sin and our acceptance with God go. If I spend the whole of my life, seventy years, eighty years, in hard work for God, it would not make me one whit more acceptable to Him. I cannot win acceptance or favor with God through my hard work or devotion. I can only win acceptance with God through the life of the Lamb who was sacrificed for me. It is when I am clothed in the righteousness of Jesus Christ that God accepts me.

Noah

But I will establish my covenant with thee; and thou shalt come into the ark, thou, and thy sons, and thy wife, and thy sons' wives with thee. And of every living thing of all flesh, two of every sort shalt thou bring into the ark, to keep them alive with thee; they shall be male and female. Of the birds after their kind, and of the cattle after their kind, of every creeping thing of the ground after its kind, two of every sort shall come unto thee, to keep them alive. And take thou unto

thee of all food that is eaten, and gather it to thee; and it shall
be for food for thee, and for them. Thus did Noah; according
to all that God commanded him, so did he. Genesis 6:18–22

And they that went in, went in male and female of all flesh, as
God commanded him: and the Lord shut him in. Genesis 7:16

And every living thing was destroyed that was upon
the face of the ground, both man, and cattle, and
creeping things, and birds of the heavens; and they were
destroyed from the earth: and Noah only was left, and
they that were with him in the ark. Genesis 7:23

And God remembered Noah, and all the beasts, and all the
cattle that were with him in the ark: and God made a wind
to pass over the earth, and the waters assuaged. Genesis 8:1

What a wonderful picture of covering the ark is! Everywhere else there was the judgment of God, the curse of God, the wrath of God; but in the ark everyone was kept alive and completely hidden, except for one window up to heaven. Anyone who stepped into the ark would have been kept alive. Every animal that was in the ark was kept alive and fed. They were not fasting but they were fed, because there was food for them in the ark.

Another wonderful picture from this Old Testament example is that they were going from an old creation, under the judgment of God, to a new creation. That is absolutely true of every one of us. If we are in Christ, we are in God's ark because Christ is God's ark. If we are in Him, we are safe. It was Moody who once nearly brought the Crystal Palace down to the ground with people weeping with laughter, when he said, "Better be a fly or a bluebottle in the ark than an elephant out of it." The point is this: however small, however insignificant, however mean, however unworthy, you are alive in the ark. Outside the ark, you may be the king of creatures, the most weighty of creatures, but there is only destruction. Oh, what a picture of covering!

There is absolute safety for us in Christ. We are kept alive in Him. The Psalmist says, "He shall keep your soul alive." Many Christians know nothing but death—the encroachment of death, the inroads of death, heaviness, darkness, bondage, limitation and corruption. But in Christ, there is quickening, fulness, power and purpose. It is all in Him.

Our soul is kept in life as we learn to stay where God has put us in God's ark, in Christ. We are absolutely safe. The only way out is upwards. We have only that one great means of communion upwards to the Father, in Christ. That is all we need.

We have food in Christ. You can try to find food elsewhere; but it is only in Christ that God gives us food. When we stay in Christ, hid with Him, abiding in Christ, we are fed. I would rather have a famine in Christ and be tested to the nth degree than have everything that there is for us in Egypt; because God can keep us alive with a little bit of meal at the bottom of the barrel if we are in Christ. He can feed us with ravens if we are in Christ. We had better stay covered, because God will preserve us there and provide for us.

The believers in Christ are passing from the old creation, under judgment, to a new. The ark belongs to the new, not to the old. We are those whom God has placed in Christ, who are journeying to a new heaven and a new earth wherein dwelleth righteousness. There is judgment on everything else. Some Christians make a terrible mistake in this matter. They think their old man, their old nature, their old life and all its attendant capacities, abilities, talents and resources is something God can use and has great pleasure in. But not at all. When God judged the old creation, He judged that which was noble and good in it. It was all crucified; all rejected; all put away. So we must understand this very simple little lesson: God has Himself judged the old creation, good and bad; and it is the new creation that really matters, what we are in Christ. Our talents come back to us when they have gone through Calvary. Our resources are given back to us when they have been broken at Calvary. All the things that belong to us which make up our own original personality, when they have gone through death, burial and resurrection, are given back to us.

To be uncovered is to stay in the old creation or hanker after the old creation. To get uncovered means that, somehow or other, we are not shut in. God shut them in the ark. People are always trying to open the door or saw holes in the ark to look out. They want to see what is happening on the horizontal level. They do not like the idea of only having a window in the roof. They hanker after the old and try to resurrect it because there were some lovely things about it. That is how we get uncovered.

There is another picture of uncovering in Noah's life:

And Noah began to be a husbandman, and planted a
vineyard: and he drank of the wine, and was drunken; and
he was uncovered within his tent. And Ham, the father of

Canaan, saw the nakedness of his father, and told his two brethren without. And Shem and Japheth took a garment, and laid it upon both their shoulders, and went backward, and covered the nakedness of their father; and their faces were backward, and they saw not their father's nakedness. And Noah awoke from his wine, and knew what his youngest son had done unto him. And he said, Cursed be Canaan; a servant of servants shall he be unto his brethren. And he said, Blessed be the Lord, the God of Shem; and let Canaan be his servant. God enlarge Japheth, and let him dwell in the tents of Shem; and let Canaan be his servant. Genesis 9:20–27

Here we have another example, this time of uncovering. The ark was the picture of being covered, but here we have a picture of uncovering. Noah had done something which was utterly wrong, but the person who got himself uncovered was his son. How did he get himself uncovered? It is very simple: "Love covers a multitude of sins." That does not mean that love is a partaker of other people's sin, but "love covers a multitude of sins". You do not gloat over somebody else's fault; to talk about it inadvisably; to not only have seen their nakedness, but to pass it on. "Have you heard?

Have you heard about so-and-so?" Then we start to tell the details. We describe their uncovered state and pass on what we saw. What happens? A curse. Sometimes, Christians know when a curse comes upon them. These things were written for our instruction. "Wherefore let him that thinketh he standeth take heed lest he fall" 1 Corinthians 10:12

The two other brothers would not even look at their father's nakedness. They would not take it in. They took a garment; they walked backwards; and they covered him. The extraordinary thing is that when the old man woke up, having done something quite wrong, the Spirit of God prophesied in him and said of his younger son, "You are cursed because you have uncovered your father and you are blessed Shem and Japheth because you covered him." That is a searching word. There is not one of us who has not uncovered somebody, sometime or other. We have gone around talking about the details. What a serious thing this is!

Abraham

The land spoke of covering for Abraham; and while he was strong in faith, all was well. Two things sum up Abraham's life–the land and his seed. He had no children, and he never got possession of the land which God promised him; but he was told to stay within it. While he stayed within it, there was absolute safety and provision. On both occasions when he went out, Egypt or an Egyptian got him down. The first time a famine came and he thought, "Now, it must obviously be the right thing to go down to Egypt where there is plenty, and we will come back up into the land when it is all over." He got into trouble and got himself uncovered. He built an altar; he departed from it. The very first thing he had to do when he got back was to go to the same altar that he had built before he fell and build it again.

It was an Egyptian, also, who brought his other downfall. God said that he would have a son and Abraham believed. But after awhile, he got more and more bothered about the way that this son would be born; and finally, his wife suggested Hagar, who was an Egyptian. There was uncovering again. This time it was a matter of someone as great as Abraham getting himself uncovered by going out of the will of God.

Moses

And the Lord said unto Moses, I will do this thing also that thou hast spoken; for thou hast found favor in my sight, and I know thee by name. And he said, Show me, I pray thee, thy glory. And he said, I will make all my goodness pass before thee, and will proclaim the name of the Lord before thee; and I will be gracious to whom I will be gracious, and will show mercy on whom I will show mercy. And he said, Thou canst not see my face; for man shall not see me and live. And the Lord said, Behold, there is a place by me, and thou shalt stand upon the rock: and it shall come to pass, while my glory passeth by, that I will put thee in a cleft of the rock, and will cover thee with my hand until I have passed by: and I will take away my hand, and thou shalt see my back; but my face shall not be seen. Exodus 33:17–23

Moses, with all his knowledge, with all his experience, and with all his intimate communion with the Lord, needed to be covered in order to see the glory of God. Now Moses was not some young disciple, just saved. He was not just out of Egypt. Here was a man who had long years with God. He had seen God in the burning bush and heard God speak, almost face to face. Again and again, we read of the way God spoke to him, the way God gave him the law, gave him the commandments, and gave him the pattern of the tabernacle. But even a man with the intimate knowledge and experience of God that Moses had, had to be hid in the cleft of a rock and the hand of God (whatever that means) put over him while the glory of the Lord passed by. There is much more to this subject than being covered because of our sinfulness; there is something to do with the very nature of God, Himself.

Tabernacle

Moreover thou shalt make the tabernacle with ten curtains; of fine twined linen, and blue, and purple, and scarlet, with cherubim the work of the skilful workman shalt thou make them. Exodus 26:1

And thou shalt make curtains of goats' hair for a tent over the tabernacle; eleven curtains shalt thou make them. Exodus 26:7

And thou shalt make a covering for the tent of rams' skins dyed red, and a covering of sealskins above. Exodus 26:14

This matter of covering is so essential that for the meeting place between God and man, there had to be four sets of covering. First, over the whole were porpoise skins. The Revised Version says sealskins, and the Authorized Version says badger skins. We can rule out the badger skins because we know that badgers never existed in the Middle East. At one time seals did come to the Sinai, but it is much more likely to be a creature called the dugong. It is a kind of porpoise that comes up the Red Sea and they use the skin, even today, in the Red Sea ports for the soles of shoes. That is how long lasting it is. So first of all, right over the whole there is something that is really weather proof, that stops the sun and other bad weather from getting in. Underneath the porpoise skins were rams' skins, tanned red. Under that was goats' hair, like a cashmere shawl. Goats' hair is very, very soft and beautiful. Beneath that was the beautiful inner curtain that could be seen on the inside–the fine twined linen, blue, purple and scarlet. These are the coverings for a place where man met with God, and they had different meanings.

Absolute Safety: First of all, there is absolute safety in Christ–something that keeps out all ills. Do you know the Lord Jesus like that as your covering? Do you know Him as the means by which all ills are kept from you so that you can persevere, so that you can endure? You are being kept alive.

Atonement: Then underneath we have atonement, which is the ram. Atonement!

Cancellation: What about the goats' hair? Someone says that speaks of atonement too. Yes; but there is something even more wonderful, which is cancellation. Do you remember the two goats? One was slain and your sins died with him; and the other went out over the horizon, carrying your sins away. He was the scapegoat. This is justification, which means that your sins are out of God's sight–carried away as far as the east is from the west.

Perfection of Christ:

- Fine twined linen–Purity
- Blue–Absolute Heavenliness (His origin)

- Purple–Royalty
- Scarlet–Redemption

Another picture of covering in the same tabernacle is that you never saw a bit of wood in the whole place. It was all covered. Inside the actual tent of meeting, every bit of wood was covered with pure gold. The wood speaks of humanity; but the gold speaks of God's nature and life of being clothed upon with Christ. Isn't that wonderful?

Another thing I would just like to mention, which I am not even going to try and explain or interpret, is the mercy seat and, above it, the cherubim. Their wings covered it completely. Why? Their faces did not look up, their faces looked down; and their wings covered it–touching. Why? Covering!

The Priest's Garments

And thou shalt make holy garments for Aaron thy brother, for glory and for beauty. And thou shalt speak unto all that are wisehearted, whom I have filled with the spirit of wisdom, that they make Aaron's garments to sanctify him, that he may minister unto me in the priest's office. And these are the garments which they shall make: a breastplate, and an ephod, and a robe, and a coat of checker work, a mitre, and a girdle: and they shall make holy garments for Aaron thy brother, and his sons, that he may minister unto me in the priest's office. And they shall take the gold, and the blue, and the purple, and the scarlet, and the fine linen. Exodus 28:2–5

And for Aaron's sons thou shalt make coats, and thou shalt make for them girdles, and head-tires shalt thou make for them, for glory and for beauty. And thou shalt put them upon Aaron thy brother, and upon his sons with him, and shalt anoint them, and consecrate them, and sanctify them, that they may minister unto me in the priest's office. And thou shalt make them linen breeches to cover the flesh of their nakedness; from the loins even unto the thighs they shall reach: and they shall be upon Aaron, and upon his sons, when they go in unto the tent of meeting, or when they come near unto the altar to minister in the holy place; that they bear not iniquity, and die: it shall be a statute for ever unto him and unto his seed after him. Exodus 28:40–43

How many believers come into the presence of the Lord without the garments of salvation on? They are ours; but we have left them and we come in our own clothes. Yet every one of us is a priest unto God; and for every single one of us, garments of salvation have been provided. We must deliberately put them on. I don't know what people do when they come into a meeting and bow their heads. What do you do?

I remember once, when I was a boy, someone next to me bowed their head and I was horrified to hear them say, "Lord, for what I am about to receive, make me truly thankful." Of course, it was true in one way; they were there for spiritual food. But I am quite sure they had forgotten; it was just a tradition. People don't know what they ought to do. They just come in and bow their heads. Their minds are thinking about who they have just seen downstairs or some problem from work or something else. What do you do when you come in? In the old days, people deliberately bowed their heads and said: "Lord, I am putting on the garments of salvation. I don't dare to come into Your presence in what I am, but I come in what Christ is. Here I am, hidden in Him." Absolutely covered. There are garments of salvation, garments of righteousness, garments of holiness, garments of praise.

Once you know you are covered, you start praising. The thing that robs us of all praise is a sense of uncleanness or not being acceptable. We cannot praise the Lord the moment we feel that we are not really acceptable to God; but, the moment we put on the garments of salvation, praise wells up in our hearts because we love our Lord for making such provision for us. We cannot help but praise Him when we see it like that. These garments are before God for glory and for beauty.

Negative Examples of Covering

Miriam and Aaron

Now we are going to look at one or two negative examples of covering. The first one is in Numbers 12:1–15, and it is the story of Miriam and Aaron. Miriam and Aaron fell out with Moses and they made a charge or accusation which was absolutely well-founded. The extraordinary thing was that God refused to take their side, and they suffered very, very greatly. Now we must ask ourselves, why? Moses had taken an Egyptian woman for a wife. However, she may have been an Egyptian who had become a convert. There were such people. The Bible deliberately says she was a Cushite, from Ethiopia; she was a very dark-skinned lady.

Hath the Lord indeed spoken only with Moses? hath he not
spoken also with us? And the Lord heard it. Numbers 12:2

It was their attitude and the words they used which uncovered them. God was quite capable of dealing with His servant, Moses; but, evidently, there was something else that was the root of this problem. All three of them had been very greatly used; there was no doubt about that. Suddenly, they came to this point and this was the result:

And the cloud removed from over the Tent; and, behold,
Miriam was leprous, as white as snow: and Aaron
looked upon Miriam, and behold, she was leprous.
And Aaron said unto Moses, Oh my lord, lay not, I
pray thee, sin upon us, for that we have done foolishly,
and for that we have sinned. Numbers 12:10–11

Isn't this an extraordinary story? Miriam was a very godly woman–a prophetess. Aaron was a godly man–high priest. What they put their finger on, in one way (as far as the Cushite side) was right; but what they said was absolutely wrong. They were touching the Lord's order and the Lord's anointed, without even realizing it. They were anointed, but so was Moses. In challenging Moses, they were challenging God; and they did not know it. They uncovered themselves. Oh, how easy it is to uncover ourselves, even when we have been greatly used of God. What does it mean: "She became leprous"? She was unclean. Something came in that made her unfit and unclean in the house of God. Sin! Thank God it ended happily because the Lord healed her; but it was uncovering. Many believers have done this kind of thing by challenging the order of God, or challenging the anointing of God. It is a terrible thing.

Korah's Rebellion

We read in Numbers sixteen about Korah's rebellion. Korah and the whole company, Dathan, Abiram, and the two hundred fifty, were all Levites. They were not just ordinary saints; they were Levites. They were not priests; but they were not just the ordinary saints. They had a lot to do with the house of God and with ministry to the Lord.

It is perfectly clear that there was ambition and jealousy at the root of this. It was what we have often called a "ministry and position–consciousness." They wanted ministry. I have seen more groups smashed up on this matter of ministry and position than any other–people who want to have a position; people who want to have a title or handle to their name; people who want to be something and be able to feel that they have arrived. That was what was behind this, and it brought uncovering.

And Korah assembled all the congregation against them unto the door of the tent of meeting: and the glory of the Lord appeared unto all the congregation. Numbers 16:19

This man Korah was absolutely convinced of the rightness of his position. He was absolutely, one hundred per cent convinced that what he had said was right. It is even more interesting in the New English Bible that it says:

Now Dathan and Abiram, holding themselves erect, had
come out to the entrance of their tent. Numbers 16:27

There was no shame; they were absolutely convinced of their rightness. Many people think that if a person is convinced of the rightness of their cause, then they won't get uncovered because God looks on the heart and He knows they are misguided. But, what has caused the misguiding? God is God. The power of God is the power of God. The fire of God is the fire of God. You cannot play about with God.

And it came to pass, as he made an end of speaking all
these words, that the ground clave asunder that was under
them; and the earth opened its mouth, and swallowed them
up, and their households, and all the men that appertained
unto Korah, and all their goods. Numbers 16:31–32

What comes from the earth always gets swallowed up by the earth; and when you have strange fire, it is fire that destroys it. That is the way God deals with things.

Evidently, Korah, Dathan and Abiram were absolutely sure they were right. You remember what they had said to Moses at the very beginning of this thing? "You take too much upon yourself. Every member of the church or community or congregation is holy and the Lord is among them all. Why do you set yourself up above the assembly of the Lord?" I have heard this kind of thing again and again. "Aren't we all believers? Who do you think you are? Who does so-and-so think they are, asking us to do this and that and the other?" They do not think for one single moment that, maybe, God has put that person in that position. Without even knowing it, we are found fighting against the Lord and setting aside or contradicting divine order. It is the surest way to get uncovered.

Sometimes, people think: "We are all believers anyway; we all have the Spirit; we are all to be anointed; we should all have gifts; so this should be a free-for-all. Does anyone think they can tell me what to do? The Spirit of God tells me what to do." That was the sin of Korah, Dathan and Abiram. Of course, the Spirit of God must tell you what to do; but there is divine order in the church. "God has set some in the church"; "Obey them that have the rule over you"; and so on. They may be rather dimwitted, and a bit stupid, but you just be careful. We must be careful that we do not set aside divine order and find ourselves contradicting God.

It is also very interesting to note that they were convinced that this bitterness sounded so spiritual: "We are all priests; we are all holy; the Lord is among us all; we have all had the Passover Lamb; we have all come out of Egypt; we are all equals before God." All of this was so good and right. Then they said, "What is more you have not brought us into a land flowing with milk and honey." Notice that they said, "Is it a small thing that you have brought us away from a land flowing with milk and honey?" (Numbers 16:13). They inverted God's order. In other words, what they were saying was this: "Purpose! Purpose! You say God is doing something? A fox could push it over. God is not doing anything in this company. God is not doing anything here or among you.

Rubbish! Rubbish! What it really is, we have left a land flowing with milk and honey instead of being brought into a land flowing with milk and honey." Such talk brings uncovering. What is the result of it? They died. It came from the earth and the earth swallowed it up; the strange fire was consumed by fire.

> *Next day all the community of the Israelites raised complaints against Moses and Aaron and taxed them with causing the death of some of the Lord's people.* Numbers 16:41 NEB

That shows how well Korah, Dathan and Abiram had put over their case. Every one who had listened said: "Well, you know they have got something. It is absolutely right, what they are saying; it is quite Scriptural." When they saw the Lord act, they said, "This is terrible; Moses and Aaron should not have done this kind of thing." Some years ago, we saw something of the very same kind of situation. Two people came to me and said: "You have caused their death. You should have done so-and-so and so-and-so." It was the very same kind of thing. It is amazing; human nature has not changed in thousands of years. We are all the same. So what happened? Everyone who was involved in this way got uncovered. The plague came. If you listen to such things and do not disassociate yourself from them, you become involved. You, yourself, become a partaker of someone else's sin and uncover yourself.

Spies

I would like to mention the spies in Numbers thirteen, because the spies well and truly uncovered themselves. They said, "We cannot go up into the land and take it, because if we do we shall be destroyed–us and our children." Joshua and Caleb said,

"We can go up; we are perfectly able to go up." The interesting thing is that the people who thought that they would be destroyed by going over to possess the land, according to the Word of God and the promise of God, died in the wilderness. The very thing they said would happen to them in the land, happened to them in the wilderness. They uncovered themselves through unbelief, and they fell through disobedience.

Achan

I hope there is no Achan among us. Achan covered something in his tent. He dug a hole in his tent and buried three things that he had stolen from Jericho. Instead of confessing it and bringing it to the light, he uncovered not only himself, but all of Israel. That is what you and I can do if we do not walk in the light. Some people ask why Achan was stoned to death. He would not have been stoned to death if he had owned up; if, at the very beginning, he had said, "It is I." But he waited until the lot went through–one after another after another, right down to him. Joshua had to say to him: "Now then, give God the glory. The lot has come to you, Achan. What have you done?" Finally, and only then, did Achan own up. I do believe that if only he had owned up at the beginning, some mercy from God would have been shown to Achan; but he would not.

Uzzah

And David again gathered together all the chosen men of Israel, thirty thousand. And David arose, and went with all the people

*that were with him, from Baalejudah, to bring up from thence
the ark of God, which is called by the Name, even the name of
the Lord of hosts that sitteth above the cherubim. And they set
the ark of God upon a new cart, and brought it out of the house
of Abinadab that was in the hill: and Uzzah and Ahio, the sons
of Abinadab, drove the new cart. And they brought it out of
the house of Abinadab, which was in the hill, with the ark. And
David and all the house of Israel played before the Lord with
all manner of instruments made of firwood, and with harps,
and with psalteries, and with timbrels, and with castanets, and
with cymbals. And when they came to the threshing-floor of
Naeon, Uzzah put forth his hand to the ark of God, and took
hold of it; for the oxen stumbled. And the anger of the Lord
was kindled against Uzzah; and God smote him there for his
error; and there he died by the ark of God.* II Samuel 6:1–7

Often, I find Christians terribly upset about this incident.
Here was a man bringing the ark of the Lord, the ark of the
covenant, back from alien territory, where it had been seized
by Philistines. The oxen became restive, the ark slid and he ran
forward to push it back on. The Lord smote him and he died.
The New English Bible says "for his rash act". God never, ever,
judges anyone without cause. If you think that dear old Uzzah
was a dear sweet believer, sensitive to the Lord and all that,
it was not so! Rashness does not go with the fear of God. The "rash
act" meant that there was no fear of the Lord in his eyes. To him,
bringing back the ark of the covenant was just a job.

"It is just a job that we do for the king. We are Levites as well,
of course." It should never have been on a cart. If it had been

on their shoulders, as God had instructed, it never would have happened. So there are many things we can think of in connection with this story; but I think what I would like to underline is that there was no fear of the Lord. Many believers put their hand out to steady the ark of the Lord. I see more people uncover themselves in this matter, perhaps than any other. They think something has happened; they think they must rush forward and push the ark back on to the cart. Nearly always, there comes uncovering. The result of the uncovering is spiritual paralysis and death.

Job

> And it was so, that, after the Lord had spoken these words unto Job, the Lord said to Eliphaz the Temanite, My wrath is kindled against thee, and against thy two friends; for ye have not spoken of me the thing that is right, as my servant Job hath. Now therefore, take unto you seven bullocks and seven rams, and go to my servant Job, and offer up for yourselves a burnt-offering; and my servant Job shall pray for you; for him will I accept, that I deal not with you after your folly; for ye have not spoken of me the thing that is right, as my servant Job hath. Job 42:7–8

Any of you who know the story of Job must surely be a little surprised, because some of these speeches of these three friends of Job's, which revealed their insight and understanding, were among the most wonderful in the Bible. But sometimes, I find myself unable to take some of these wonderful sayings from these gentlemen because of this verse. However, I find some of them among the most wonderful in the Bible. And some of the things Job said are, in my estimation, some of the most terrible things in the whole Bible. He said to the Lord: "You are playing a cat-and-mouse game with me. You are just trying to tear me to pieces. You are trying to corner me. Who are you? If you were an ordinary person I would take you to law." If you read it in the New English Bible or in Moffet, you will be shocked at some of the things Job said. Now, at the beginning, Job never said anything. When the calamity fell upon Job, his sons died, his oxen died, everything was taken from him; but he bowed down and worshiped the Lord and said: "The Lord has given and the Lord has taken away. Blessed be the name of the Lord." Then he went and sat on a dung heap. His three friends came to see him and, for the first blessed seven days, they kept their mouths shut; but not for long. Watching the misery and agony of Job, they could bear it no longer. They began with those marvelous speeches where they traveled all around the world, explored the solar system, traveled over the whole universe, plumbed the seas, became amateur botanists, zoologists, biologists, geologists, weathermen, and the lot. They all came back to one thing: "Job, you have sinned." And slowly, bit by bit, they got Job to uncover himself.

Oh, how we do this to one another. When someone has a calamity to fall upon them which cannot be explained, there are dear believers who keep their mouths shut a few hours, sometimes a few days, sometimes a week; and then, finally, they can bear it no longer. In they come with all colors flying to put them right: "It was this and this and this; God is showing you. We knew it; we saw it coming. You had to go this way." Finally, they are prodded into a place where they have to say something; and then as they go on, they find themselves saying the most terrible things.

In actual fact, the Lord smiled, not at the three friends, but at Job. "Oh," said the Lord, "you would take me to court, would you?" Finally, the Lord came to Job and said to him, out of the whirlwind: "Job, I want to ask you a question. Why did I create the hippopotamus?" It is a good question, isn't it? Job had no answer, but the lesson went on. "Job, you don't understand. There are things beyond your understanding." Job said: "I have said too much. I will say no more." And he bowed before the Lord. You would have thought that Job was the one who had been uncovered, but the Lord said: "No, I understand my dear servant Job. It was an evil spirit; it was Satan who did all this to him to prove him. It certainly brought out a lot and I understand my servant Job. But these other three, who have put together such marvelous sermons, Spurgeon–like sermons, things that would have filled the Westminister Chapel with their brilliance, have not said the thing that is right from Me. They have uncovered themselves and unless they quickly offer up a sacrifice and get Job to pray for them, there will be trouble." The three did the wise thing. They rushed off, got a sacrifice and asked Job if he would pray for them; and the matter was put right. There is a little lesson here for all of us. Sometimes, when a person is under the dealings of God, we can start to try and help and, in so doing, get ourselves uncovered.

Hezekiah

II Kings 20:12–21

Dear old Hezekiah was such a man of God. He had seen God's victories; he had seen the Lord coming in a mighty way. Then the Babylonian ambassador came to dinner. They were talking about the beauty of the palace and Hezekiah got carried away and said, "Oh, you haven't seen anything; come with me." He took him right into all the vaults of the treasury and said, "Look at all this; look at this and this." The Babylonian ambassador was absolutely impressed. "Marvelous, absolutely marvelous." And Hezekiah said, "We are not such a small little state after all, are we? We are something." Yes, the Babylonian ambassador was deeply impressed. But when he went out, the prophet of the Lord said to Hezekiah: "You have done an evil thing. Because you have done this thing, Babylon shall come and take all these treasures away, not in your lifetime, but in your son's lifetime." Unwittingly, Hezekiah had uncovered himself and the people of God. How had he done it? I suppose we would say that it was really the "casting of pearl before swine". He had absolutely no business showing the treasures of God to the enemies of God. Some of us need to learn that simple little lesson. Pride! Oh, what God has done for us; then suddenly, we start to talk about it in a way as if it is all us. We can talk about a work such as this and its history in a way that suggests we are wonderful people, that we are marvelous people, and that this is because we are here. Without even realizing it, we have uncovered ourselves.

Uzziah

II Chronicles 26:4,5,16–21

Uzziah was a jolly good king and it actually says of him that he sought the Lord for understanding and wisdom, and the Lord blessed him very greatly. But then it says that when he became great, he was corrupted. How did this corruption come? He went into the house of the Lord with a censer and went into the holy place. He was the king. The high priest went to him and said, "You have not done the thing that is right; not even a king is permitted to come into this place." Uzziah was angry and instantly became a leper. He went out from the presence of the Lord into a separate house and was not even buried in the royal tomb. How is it possible for a man who was so greatly used of God, who was such a godly man, to end up uncovered? Yet I am afraid to say that it is possible. That is why we must all remember the word: "Wherefore let him that thinketh he standeth take heed lest he fall."

David and Bathsheba and the Numbering of Israel

It was at the time when kings go forth to war, but not David. He stayed at home and while sitting on the roof, perhaps composing a Psalm, playing the lute or the lyre, he saw Bathsheba bathing herself on a roof. At that moment, temptation became sin. Now this is the interesting thing.

The Lord Jesus taught us in the pattern prayer to pray: "Lead us not into temptation, but deliver us from the evil one." In other words, if David had been out in the forefront of the battle, where he should have been, it would not have happened.

Satan stood up against Israel and tempted David to number them. One version says Satan stood up; the other version says God moved David to do it. So it shows that, sometimes, God allows Satan to do something, as He did with Peter: "Satan has obtained thee by request." After the numbering of the people took place, there was a terrible plague. But the wonderful thing in these incidences to do with David is that, when confessed, both of them became part of the purpose of God. From Bathsheba was born Solomon and Nathan; and from the numbering of the people, when it was confessed and put right, David found the site for the house of God, the place where the house of God was to be built.

The Man of God and the Old Prophet

1 Kings 13:1–32

This is an extraordinary story. This man of God was so faithful. He had come from Judah to Bethel in the Northern Kingdom. He stood by the altar, which was a false altar, and he uttered the Word of God, a prophecy–God would destroy that place and take the whole nation into captivity. The old prophet had also been used of God, but had evidently become a bit lethargic in his old age. He heard from his sons about the man of God and his prophecy and he said he would like to go and see him. He went to see him and said to the man of God, "Do come and have a meal with us." "No," said the man of God, "I cannot do that because God told me not to eat anything nor to take any drink on my journey; only to come in and to go out and not even greet anyone." "Oh," lied the old prophet, "but God has spoken to me as well. He has told me you should come to me for a meal." He persuaded the man of God, who went in for a meal with the old prophet. Suddenly, during the course of the meal, the old prophet prophesied and said: "You have been disobedient to the Lord. You shall not be buried in the sepulchre of your fathers." The man of God saddled his ass, went out, and a lion met him in the way and killed him. Disobedience! You can fulfill a ministry and be disobedient. Oh, may God preserve us from all these things.

Thank God for the Ark in which we are safe. Thank God for the Lamb whose blood has cleansed us and with whose righteousness we are clothed. Thank God for the Tabernacle hidden; our life hid with Christ in God. Thank God for the garments of salvation, the garments of praise

There is no need to be uncovered; but may every single one of us take note of these solemn instances of uncovering, as well as covering. These things were written for our instruction, our education and our admonition, upon whom the ends of the ages have come. "Wherefore let him that thinketh he standeth take heed lest he fall."

Shall we pray:

Dear Lord, Thou knowest these things are solemn and we are dealing with things of which not just the young ones among us need to take note, but of which the eldest among us need to take note. Oh Father, we pray together that we shall learn some of these lessons and may learn how to abide in Christ, how to know what it is to have our life hid with Christ in Thee. Oh, by Thy Holy Spirit, keep us from uncovering ourselves in any way at all. Lead us, we pray, Father, not into temptation, but deliver us from the evil one. We ask it together in the name of our Lord Jesus Christ. Amen.

7.
Mystery of Covering

Isaiah 4:2–6

In that day shall the branch of the Lord be beautiful and glorious, and the fruit of the land shall be excellent and comely for them that are escaped of Israel. And it shall come to pass, that he that is left in Zion, and he that remaineth in Jerusalem, shall be called holy, even every one that is written among the living (book of life) in Jerusalem; when the Lord shall have washed away the filth of the daughters of Zion, and shall have purged the blood of Jerusalem from the midst thereof, by the spirit of justice, and by the spirit of burning. And the Lord will create over the whole habitation of mount Zion, and over her assemblies, a cloud and smoke by day, and the shining of a flaming fire by night; for over all the glory shall be spread a covering. And there shall be a pavilion for a shade in the day-time from the heat, and for a refuge and for a covert from storm and from rain.

Shall we pray?

Oh beloved Lord, we thank Thee for those wonderful words we have sung: "My name, from the palms of His hands, eternity will not erase. Impressed on His heart it remains in marks of indelible grace." Oh, how we thank Thee, our beloved Father, for putting us in the Lord Jesus Christ; for the security, the eternal security which is ours in Him. Father, we pray that, by Thy Spirit, Thou wilt make this time life-giving; a time of illumination; a time of divine revelation; a time when things that, perhaps we know in the head become, somehow, known in the heart; when things dawn on us in all their wonder and power and glory. Oh, Father, we pray that Thou will not allow these studies on this matter of covering to just, somehow, pass us by, to become just one more study which we have gone through; but rather Lord, we pray that we may be a people who know in our experience what it is to abide in the Lord. Hear us then, Lord, as we commit ourselves to Thee, the weakness of these lips and the weakness of this mind and body. Thou art able, Lord, to display Thy superior power and grace and Thou canst, Lord, through the anointing upon our Lord Jesus Christ, cause this speaking and ministry to be anointed and that our hearing also be anointed. We ask it in His name. Amen.

There is so much to this matter of covering. How do you explain a mystery when it remains a mystery? It is just marvelous when a mystery has been revealed; but there are some things which still remain a mystery, and I can only lead you so far. At a first reading and a superficial reading of the Bible concerning this matter of covering, it would seem that it is all to do with sin and failing. In other words, we think of Adam and Eve. They sinned and they were immediately conscious that they were naked. God shed blood and clothed them, covered them with skin. Most of us have a deep-seated conception of this matter as being something to do, essentially, with sin. If there had been no sin, there would be no need of covering. We are sinners and we need the garment of salvation; we need to be robed with the robe of His righteousness; we have no hope of coming before God except in Christ. It is virtually a question of knowing how to confess sin, how to take Christ as our salvation and our righteousness and our acceptance before God. Nevertheless, as we go deeper into this whole matter in the Word of God, we discover that it has far greater meaning and significance. In fact, we begin to discover that this matter of covering is not just to do with sin and human failing. It appears that before sin ever entered the world, there was, evidently, some kind of need for covering.

The Covering Cherub

In the Word of God, there are only one or two Scriptures on this matter.

> *Thou wast the anointed cherub that covereth: and I set thee, so that thou wast upon the holy mountain of God; thou hast walked up and down in the midst of the stones of fire. Thou was perfect in thy ways from the day that thou wast created, till unrighteousness was found in thee. By the abundance of thy traffic they filled the midst of thee with violence, and thou hast sinned: therefore have I cast thee as profane out of*

the mountain of God; and I have destroyed thee, O covering
cherub, from the midst of the stones of fire. Ezekiel 28:14–16

This is the extraordinary prophecy concerning Satan and how he fell. The devil has been called here "the cherub that covereth"; and then again in verse 16 "the covering cherub". The Hebrew word here is one of the three translated in English by the word cover; and it is the word, in this instance, "to hedge in" or "to enclose". There is the thought here of this person hedging in something or enclosing something, protecting or guarding something. He was the guardian; he was the protector. This was before sin ever entered into the world. This was before there was the whole story of the fall, before unrighteousness was found even in Lucifer. This verse was so problematical that the Revised Standard Version translated it or amended it to this: "With the anointed cherub I placed you." Then they put a note and said: "Hebrew quite obscure. I cast you as a profane thing from the mountain of God and the guardian cherub drove you out" (v.16). That is how they have amended it. There is something extraordinary here. Someone is called (if we take the Hebrew literally) "the anointed cherub that covereth", and that doesn't seem to make too much sense.

What was it that God gave Satan or Lucifer to do? What was his job? We look back into the mists before time was and we get a glimpse of someone whose job was covering, who had something to do with the glory of God and something to do with the presence of God. This one was anointed by God to guard, to protect, to cover, to hedge in or to enclose. The New English Bible follows the Revised Standard Version in amending it, in exactly the same way, by suggesting that an anointed cherub was with this person, and so on. To the human mind, it just doesn't seem to make sense, so it has been amended in a way that would seem or appear to make sense. But that is never the way with the Word of God—to amend it so that it falls in with our understanding or sense.

Covering over the Glory of God

And the Lord will create over the whole habitation of mount Zion, and over her assemblies, a cloud and smoke by day, and the shining of a flaming fire by night; for over all the glory shall be spread a covering. Isaiah 4:5

Have you ever heard that the glory of God needs a covering? Again, this Hebrew word here means, very simply, "covering" or "canopy", or as the Authorized Version puts it, "defense". The Hebrew word does not mean defense, but it has the thought of overlaying something, thus protecting it; so the old Authorized Version translators and the King James translators translated the word "for a defense", not incorrectly. This covering of glory is for a defense, overlaying it. I suggest to you that we are face to face with mystery. Why is there a need for there to be a covering over the glory when there is no more sin and no more Satan in eternity to come, in the ages to come; when all that is evil has finally been finished and done away with, burned up in the lake of fire? Why is there a need for there to be an overlaying over the glory? Why a canopy? The Revised Standard Version uses the word canopy. The Septuagint, which is the earliest Greek version that we have, puts it this way:

Yea, there shall be, as it were, the smoke and light of fire
burning by night and upon all the glory shall be a defense.

Once again, the New English Bible has found it far too much.
It just didn't make sense to our modern translators and, therefore,
this is how they have rendered it: For glory shall be spread over
all as a covering and a canopy.... Of course, we must all say,
immediately, that makes much more sense. We have to say that
that falls completely into line with all that we know. There is a
note which tells us that the Hebrew is obscure. But the Hebrew
is not obscure! Our understanding of the Hebrew is obscure.
The Hebrew is here and it is perfectly clear. In verse 5, it says,
"And the Lord will create over the whole habitation of mount
Zion, and over her assemblies, a cloud and smoke by day, and the
shining of a flaming fire by night; for over all the glory shall be
spread a covering" (Isaiah 4:5).

That little preposition over is precisely the same word used
in modern Hebrew for on. If I put something on a table, if I put
something over something, it is exactly the same. "On the glory
there shall be a covering." There is no mystery about it; the mystery
is what it means. Again and again, our more modern translators
feel that if there is anything which does not add up, it means that
the original is obscure. They feel that some dreadful mistake
has been made by some sleepy copyist who fell asleep when he
was copying and changed a Hebrew letter or two. So, there must
be something obscure here; therefore, they ought to amend it.
But, in fact, it is quite simple: "Over the glory, a covering."

What does that mean? I have provoked a whole number of
questions, and left you in midair. But I have to say that I do not

know what it means, except that we are touching something which is not just to do with sin and human failing. It is something that was, evidently, an essential need when there was no sin and no failing; and, one day, when there is no more sin and no more human failing, there will still be a need.

For I, saith the Lord, will be unto her a wall of fire round about, and I will be the glory in the midst of her. Zechariah 2:5

Cherubim and Seraphim

In the tabernacle, where the glory of the Lord filled the whole place, there was a veil; and on that veil, which spoke of the absolute holiness of God, were embroidered cherubim. "The anointed cherub that covereth ... " He fell. In Genesis, chapter 3, it was a cherubim, a sort of flame, that stood guarding the way to the tree of life. You see it in the tabernacle and in the temple. When you go into the holiest place of all, you see two huge cherubim on the mercy seat. These cherubim in the temple were so great that their wing span together was from end to end, from wall to wall. What does it all mean? Again, it seems to have something to do with covering. It says their wings cover. Their wings covered the mercy seat and the Ark of the covenant, which was the outward symbol of the presence of God. Those great wings were covering something. The glory of the Lord appeared there. It was there that God communed with the high priest. Again, there is something here that I cannot fully understand the mystery of covering.

And under the firmament were their wings straight,
the one toward the other: every one had two which
covered on this side, and every one had two which
covered on that side, their bodies. Ezekiel 1:23

And their faces and their wings were separate above;
two wings of every one were joined one to another,
and two covered their bodies. Ezekiel 1:11

These cherubim and their wings are quite extraordinary. Whoever sees the cherubim is always struck by their wings. A little farther on in Ezekiel, a most extraordinary thing happens in this vision. As the prophet Ezekiel looks at the cherubim, a man's hand appears under the wing and, in one case, the hand comes out and takes coals from off the altar. It struck them all.

When we come to the last book of the Bible, Revelation 4, these strange creatures are there again the four living creatures full of eyes and we hear, again, that they have these wings. We are told there that they have three pairs of wings six wings each of them in perpetual motion, and they are crying, "Holy, holy, holy, is the Lord God Almighty."

In Isaiah 6, in the year King Uzziah died and Isaiah saw the Lord sitting upon a throne, high and lifted up, he saw seraphim. Some people have tried to tell us that seraphim are angels, but I side with rabbinical scholarship in this matter, who, without exception, all say that the seraphim are like the cherubim. They are, in fact, symbolic. These seraphim here have six wings with two they cover the face (which is a most extraordinary thing), with two they cover their feet, and with two they fly.

Have you ever seen creatures fly with two wings over their eyes, two wings over their feet, and with two they fly? What does it mean, that whenever we see the presence of the Lord or the glory of the Lord, we see these cherubim? It is as if they speak of the whole creation of God, in its entirety, visible and invisible, everything as the expression of the glory and grace and power of God. We saw them within the holiest place and on the veil, both in the tabernacle and in the temple.

The Majesty of God

> *For our God is a consuming fire. Hebrews 12:29*

There are those who would like to relegate that to the Old Testament. They seem to think that God was only a consuming fire in the Old Testament, that He has changed His character since then and has now become a sort of gentle, old man. But the writer of the Hebrews says, "Our God is a consuming fire." That is His character; that is His nature. He is a consuming fire. He has just been speaking about receiving a kingdom that cannot be shaken. He is speaking about giving service, well pleasing to God, with reverence and awe. Why? Because "our God is a consuming fire."

> *For the Lord thy God is a devouring fire,*
> *a jealous God. Deuteronomy 4:24*

> *The sinners in Zion are afraid; trembling hath seized the godless one: whom among us can dwell with the devouring fire? who among us can dwell with everlasting burnings? Isaiah 33:14*

And the Lord said, Behold, there is a place by me, and thou shalt stand upon the rock: and it shall come to pass, while my glory passeth by, that I will put thee in a cleft of the rock, and will cover thee with my hand until I have passed by: and I will take away my hand, and thou shalt see my back; but my face shall not be seen. Exodus 33:21,23

The majesty of God, the infinite greatness of God, the infinite power and holiness of God, what the old Puritans called "the unutterable holiness of God" are not appreciated today. You have to go a long, long way in Christian circles to hear someone preach on the majesty of God. We are often left, even in Christian circles, with the feeling that God is very cozy, very small, very little. Somehow, we have managed to make God smaller, at least in our conception. We have reduced Him. We have made Him more mundane, more ordinary, more cozy, and more easily analyzed. We can inspect God. We can put Him under a kind of spiritual microscope and examine Him. We can almost take Him apart and put Him together again, and I sometimes think they do in some theological seminaries. We categorize His attributes and pigeonhole everything about Him so that, in the end, instead of being left with a sense of the infinite and greatness of God, and how awe inspiring He is, we are left with someone who we have managed to analyze and have at our fingertips. But God is God eternally and unchangeably the same.

There was no more nonsensical teaching than that teaching which told us that the God who appeared to our fathers at Sinai is today a changed character: then He was all fire and now He is all mercy; He revealed Himself as fire then and reveals Himself in this age as love. But, to imagine that He has changed His character, as if God can evolve in a kind of spiritual Darwinian theory of divine evolution, or that He evolved from some tribal patriarchal deity who was savage and cold and full of law to a God who is benign and loving and sweet, is nonsensical. No wonder many young people in the world have turned away from the idea of a God like that some old gentleman up in the sky. God is no old gentleman up in the sky. The God who caused Mt. Sinai to smoke like a furnace is the same God you and I have come to know through Jesus Christ. He is no different. He is a consuming fire, infinite in power, infinite in majesty, unutterably holy. That is the God with whom you and I have to do, the LIVING GOD, eternally the same.

The heaven of heavens cannot contain Him; not if there are billions and billions of universes will you exhaust Him. If there were billions multiplied by billions of universes, still beyond the end of them, God would be infinite. There is no end to His majesty. There is no end to His power. There is no end to His greatness.

If that is so, certainly it must be true that no finite created being, such as you and such as me, can ever fully comprehend Him. Do you really think you can analyze God? NO! Does that not make you think? The twentieth century has made no difference to Him; it has not limited Him. The fact that we explore space, that we have whizzed around one of the smaller of His planets, that we are trying to do this and that, has not made it any more difficult for God. With one word, He could finish the whole thing. He is absolutely the same! It has not made it harder for Him or easier for Him. He is the same.

Do you begin to see how wonderful it is that God became man? God, so infinite in His majesty and in His power, became a man born of a simple human being and he came to us in such a way that He is located, that He is understood, that He has a color to His hair, a color to His eyes, He has skin, flesh and blood, and a body like you and me. The wonder of the resurrection and ascension of Christ is that, today, He has a body. He is not some ethereal being at the right hand of God the Father, but he is a Person with an actual body who, one day, by the grace of God, if He so allow us, we shall be able to touch. He is a human being, still God, but also Man; so that this Person, infinite in majesty, infinite in wisdom, infinite in power and unutterably holy can be understood by you and me. We can know an intimate relationship to Him. We can know Him as "Abba, Father". But woe betide any of us who, having been introduced into such an intimate relationship with God, should start to become familiar. God is love, but God is also power, and truth, and righteousness, and holiness.

This means, simply, that if the glory of God were to break out upon us, it would be as if we were touched by a million volts. We would shrivel up. That is why, in the Old Testament, again and again, there is this strange word: "Lest I break out upon them". What a strange thing to say. "Tell them to keep their distance, tell them to stand away, lest I break out upon them and they die." We have enough in the Old Testament to understand what the presence of God can do.

Apart from human failing and sin, we still need to be covered. There needs to be an overlaying of the glory. There needs to be a protection of the glory at least, I humbly submit this as a possible explanation for some of these verses. In Christ, you and I approach the infinite power and holiness of God, and we are absolutely safe. Oh, the privilege that is ours! When people become familiar with God, when you hear His name bandied about, when you hear Him spoken of as if He is some commodity to be sold, some sort of trite experience to be tried, doesn't it hurt you? I can never understand Christians who don't get sensitive or hurt. I suppose I am an old-fashioned, antiquarian sort of person; but I find there is nothing more wonderful in the whole world than when people are full of the Spirit and full of Christ, when the language is genuine because it is all about Him, and when there is a sharing. I don't know whether it is me, but sometimes, when I go around the country, I find it is a battle all the time to stop myself from shriveling up. I hear things, I see things and I sometimes think, "Dear Lord, I feel so sorry for You; are You here at Your table?" Here is someone dressed in such a slovenly way that you would not think they had come to anyone but the dustman. And here is someone whose posture is so familiar, so cheap, that you would think they were watching the television in some dirty little back room somewhere. Or, here is language which is far from being correct. We cannot all speak with an Oxford accent, and God forbid that we should, but the fact still remains there is a sense of God's dignity when we speak. I have heard people with a Cockney accent speak of the Lord and speak to Him in such a way as to bring tears to your eyes and warm your heart. It is because they are conscious that they are in the presence of a Person infinite in power and infinite in grace.

How would you like it if someone you loved very much was being offered as a kind of commodity? "Why don't you try Him?", you hear. Are they speaking about that Person who means so much to me? No wonder Malcom Muggeridge said a year or two ago on television that he could not understand evangelicals because they spoke of God as if He were a thing rather than a Person.

We can all become so familiar with the Lord that we fall into a kind of jargon, into a kind of phraseology where it just seems as if the fact that we are in a living union with a person has taken a backseat; and now it is a thing, a power, something impersonal. I just simply want to say here that God is still God. His power and His glory are still exactly the same. Just because we have become familiar with the Lord or we have come to know Him in a very intimate and wonderful way through Christ, does not mean for one single instant that He is different. One day, you and I will see the Lord with our eyes. In our flesh, we shall see God.

It seems to me that this whole matter of covering is not just to do with sin and with failing, but it is something to do with the Person and the infinite power of that Person. If we were to understand this, the fear of the Lord, which is the beginning of wisdom, would come upon us all. I only pray that this time may serve that end. We cannot understand this subject fully. All we know is that we are touching a mystery.

Moses said, "May I see Your glory?" And God said to the one person in that day and age that He knew most intimately and most wonderfully: "You shall see it. You shall stand by Me upon this rock and My glory shall pass you by. As I pass by you, I will cover you with My hand in the cleft of the rock. My back you shall see but My face you shall not see." People tell me that Moses did not know anything about the substitutionary death of the Lord Jesus, the atoning death of the Lord Jesus. I think it is nonsense. The blood of animals had already been shed. Typically, he was as much covered as you and I by the blood of those creatures. They were looking forward. It was a question of glory. therefore, it is simply wonderful that in Revelation 22, it says, "They shall see His face." How marvelous that will be to see the face of God.

Don't think that this subject is some small thing just to do with our sin and failing, as great as that would be. It is something much, much bigger. Oh, how wonderful it is that God loves us. How amazing it is that this infinite God should long for our fellowship and should long to dwell with us. It is incredible that He should have gone to such lengths to obtain us. I think it is amazing. "Amazing grace, how sweet the sound, that saved a wretch like me."

Shall we pray:

Oh Lord, this whole matter is beyond us; but by Thy Spirit, would Thou impress us with something of the profoundness of it and the mystery of it, so that we may be a people who come to know Thee intimately, who experience all that Thou hast given us in the Lord Jesus Christ, and yet, at the same time, never become cheap and never become familiar. Oh Father, grant we pray, for every one of us, that we might know that in our experience; and we may know what it is, Lord, to remain covered. We ask it in the name of our Lord Jesus. Amen.

8.
The Testimony of Sisters to Covering

1 Corinthians 11:2–16

Now I praise you that ye remember me in all things, and hold fast the traditions, even as I delivered them to you. But I would have you know, that the head of every man is Christ; and the head of the woman is the man; and the head of Christ is God. Every man praying or prophesying, having his head covered, dishonoreth his head. But every woman praying or prophesying with her head unveiled dishonoreth her head; for it is one and the same thing as if she were shaven. For if a woman is not veiled, let her also be shorn: but if it is a shame to a woman to be shorn or shaven, let her be veiled. For a man indeed ought not to have his head veiled, forasmuch as he is the image and glory of God: but the woman is the glory of the man. For the man is not of the woman; but the woman of the man: for neither was the man created for the woman; but the woman for the man: for this cause ought the woman to have a sign of authority on her head, because of the angels. Nevertheless, neither is the woman without the man, nor the man without the woman, in the Lord. For as the woman is of the man, so is the man also by the woman; but all things are of God. Judge ye in yourselves: is it seemly that a woman pray unto God unveiled? Doth not even nature itself teach you, that, if a man have long hair, it is a dishonor to him? But if a woman have long hair, it is a glory to her: for her hair is given her for a covering. But if any man seemeth to be contentious, we have no such custom, neither the churches of God.

Genesis 2:18–25

And the Lord God said, It is not good that the man should be alone; I will make him a help meet for him. And out of the ground the Lord God formed every beast of the field, and every bird of the heavens; and brought them unto the man to see what he would call them: and whatsoever the man called every living creature, that was the name thereof. And the man gave names to all cattle, and to the birds of the heavens, and to every beast of the field; but for man there was not found a help meet for him. And the Lord God caused a deep sleep to fall upon the man, and he slept; and he took one of his ribs, closed up the flesh instead thereof: and the rib, which the Lord God had taken from the man, made he a woman, and brought her unto the man. And the man said, This is now bone of my bones, and flesh of my flesh: she shall be called Woman, because she was taken out of Man. Therefore shall a man leave his father and his mother, and shall cleave unto his wife: and they shall be one flesh. And they were both naked, *the man and his wife, and were not ashamed.*

Ephesians 5:22–33

Wives, be in subjection unto your own husbands, as unto the Lord. For the husband is the head of the wife, as Christ also is the head of the church, being himself the saviour of the body. But as the church is subject to Christ, so let the wives also be to their husbands in everything. Husbands, love your wives, even as Christ also loved the church, and gave himself up for it; that he might sanctify it, having cleansed it by the washing of water with the word, that he might present the church to himself a glorious church, not having spot or wrinkle or any such thing; but that it should be holy and without blemish. Even so ought husbands also to love their own wives as their own bodies. He that loveth his own wife loveth himself: for no man ever hated his own flesh; but nourisheth and cherisheth it, even as Christ also the church; because we are members of his body. For this cause shall a man leave his father and mother, and shall cleave to his wife; and the two shall become one flesh. This mystery is great: but I speak in regard of Christ and of the church. Nevertheless do ye also severally love each one his own wife even as himself; and let the wife see that she fear her husband

Shall we pray?

Now Lord, we have asked Thee to be with us. We have together confessed and recognized our need of the Holy Spirit to lead us into all truth, and we thank Thee now, Lord, that we can just spread out our time before Thee. We believe, Lord, that Thou Thyself and Thou will take note of our cry and of our confidence in Thyself and Thou will meet us in this time. Oh Lord, hear us; take away all strain, all tension. May we just know what it is to be in Thy presence. We ask it together in the name of our Lord Jesus. Amen.

We are going to consider now perhaps the most controversial point of all in this matter of covering–the sisters, the testimony in the church to covering. Some of us may have background difficulties or we may have complexes in the matter. It is amazing how this subject brings out rebellion and resistance and many other things. I just pray that the Lord, by the Spirit, will free us from a lot of these silly things that bind us.

The Significance of Head Covering as a Sign

Unfortunately, many people approach this subject of covering by taking the matter of sisters first, and this entirely puts everyone off, particularly the sisters. We have gone the other way around and seen the whole subject as a tremendous thing, far, far bigger than any physical difference between men and women, even in the church. Now we come to this question as to whether, in fact, it is true to say that sisters are meant to be a divinely-constituted and divinely-given sign in the church to this vitally important truth.

We have a number of signs which testify to and express certain truths. For instance, we all are well aware of the sign that we see every Sunday morning, and at other times when the Lord so leads us, of the bread and the wine. We are quite clear that the bread speaks of something. It has significance; it signifies something. We are quite clear that the wine signifies something. There is a testimony within the bread itself and the wine itself to something far, far greater than either the bread or the wine, something universal in its significance and meaning.

We are all well aware of baptism. When people go down into the waters of baptism and are immersed in the water, we know that it is a symbol. Baptism itself does nothing. The waters are not magical. There is nothing supernatural about it. But in the simple ceremony, there is a sign; something is signified. The death and burial and resurrection of our Lord Jesus Christ is set forth.

The laying on of hands is a sign. It covers a whole number of things in Scripture, but in it there is a sign. There is a significance of identification with the body, or with the church, and with the risen Head as other members lay hands on us.

Anointing with oil when we are sick is another sign. The oil does not do anything. Many, many centuries ago, Zwingli, in a famous sermon in Zurich said, "Better keep your oil for salad dressing if you think that it is going to do anything to you." He was talking about extreme unction and the doctrine of rushing oil to someone who is dying so that they may get into the kingdom. But he said, "Better have it on your salad if you think that there is anything supernatural in the oil." However, the anointing of the sick person with oil is a sign; it signifies something. It signifies the health and soundness and wholeness that there is for us in the life of God, in the life of the Lord Jesus Christ, and in life through the Spirit of God.

In many senses, marriage is a sign. It signifies something much more than just two people coming together and the creation of a family and a new home. Something more is signified.

I think we are all well aware of these signs. We have no argument about that. The point we are making is that it has been given by God to the sisters in their very constitution, their behavior, their attitude, and their dress to be the perpetual reminder to the whole church of one of the most important truths in the Word of God. I find it very sad if sisters opt out of such a testimony. I find it extremely sad when sisters jam some hat upon their head without any understanding at all as to what it means. There is no glory in that. There is no real significance in just obeying a regulation anymore than there is in someone who is not really saved thinking that the waters and the rite itself will do something. So obviously, just wearing a hat, as some say "in obedience", is not going to get us very far. But oh, how wonderful it is when this matter is understood, not only by the sisters, but by the brothers. Brothers don't always help the sisters in this matter at all because they don't understand. They often think it is just a question of women shutting up and being obedient; therefore, they ought to wear a hat in that context and meaning. So you get the old battle of the sexes brought into the church with all the deep bitterness that comes from it. Freud was right, of course, when he said, "One of the deepest things in human life is the battle between the sexes." It is often very deep and very hidden. We don't often talk about it; but even within the people of God, there is this deep-seated battle–bitterness, rebellion, and many other things that come from it. This ought not to be. We are free, we are delivered, we are the people of God; and in that sense, there should be none of that at all.

All that we have studied on this matter of covering is summed up and expressed in this sign in the most remarkable way; but it is not just to do with head covering. It goes far deeper than that. The sister is a sign in her constitution, not just in the hat that she wears, or whatever she may put on her head. On few subjects has there been produced so much perplexity, misunderstanding, and, in many instances, so much bondage and bitterness. I cannot think of any subject quite like this matter. I know there are many subjects that cause tremendous difficulty and complexity, but I can think of no subject that is more perplexing, to many sisters in particular, than this matter. Certainly the most extraordinary and contradictory teachings have been deduced from these Scriptures that we have read. There are theories of adjustment and theories of accommodation, whereby you start off with something and fit the Scripture into that mold. "The twentieth century says so-and-so in the society we live in; therefore, the Scripture cannot say this. There must be something wrong." Many theories of adjustment have been propounded on the most weak, and sometime false, facts.

I have heard the most amazing theories propounded on these Scriptures. It is not unlike the enemy to have sought to obscure a glorious truth and a glorious privilege. If this is a truth in which there is glory and a privilege that has been gloriously given to some of us, then we can understand Satan coming in. He has done so with the Lord's table, with baptism, with so many things, so as to obscure the truth and to make it so perplexing and so complex that we almost throw up our hands in despair and abandon it altogether. Satan has sought to turn light into darkness. On the one hand, there are people who tell me that it is deliverance to throw away your hat-turning light into darkness. On the other hand, we find a whole section of the church has been pushed into the most abject bondage and misery by this kind of teaching–turning light into darkness, turning privilege into bondage, turning testimony into misery. I say all that because many folks, especially the ladies, cannot approach this subject without deep-seated prejudices and bias. I suppose there is no century in which it is more difficult for the ladies to approach this subject without prejudice and bias than in this day of women's lib. But here it is. We have got to face it. The Word of God is the Word of God.

False Conceptions About Head Covering

There are a number of false conceptions from which we need to be delivered. By searching the Word of God and looking to the Lord, we are going to seek to find what the Lord really has to say. Here are what I consider to be some of the false conceptions about this matter.

The Woman is Inferior

The woman is not an equal partner either in marriage or in the church. She is inferior; and indeed, the whole implication is that she is to be servile. She needs to be seen but not heard. That is a fallacy! It approaches heresy. You have only to think for a moment to recognize that a woman's soul and a woman's personality are as valuable as that of any man. There is no second-class citizen in the kingdom of God. Out of this comes much of the bitterness, the prejudice, and the bias against this whole subject; and Christian gentlemen have not always helped the sisters in this matter. It has often been put over in such a way that the sisters' deep- seated suspicion that they are being told that they are unequal and inferior is supposed to be founded in the Word of God. But it is no where found in the Word of God. That is the first thing, and the most important; because out of this has come all the bitterness and trouble on this whole matter.

Private Prayer or Sister's Meeting

> But every woman praying or prophesying with her
> head unveiled dishonoreth her head; for it is one and the
> same thing as if she were shaven. I Corinthians 11:5

We are told that this is not a church meeting; this is obviously private prayer or it is a sisters' prayer meeting. This has no foundation. In I Corinthians the apostle is dealing with church matters and church gatherings. He is speaking about the contribution of both men and women in the gathering of the church. For this reason, in some circles, a sister's hat is hardly ever removed. I remember, some years ago, my sister went to stay with a rather strict group down in Cornwall, where, to her amazement, the ladies went into the sea with their bathing costumes without, at any point, removing their hats. Then, to her even deeper amazement, she found the dear sister at the cooker with her hat on. She said, quite honestly and sincerely, from pure motive, "Well, I might be praying." This is very interesting, because in orthodox Jewish circles this is why orthodox Jewish men keep something on their heads the whole time, lest at any given moment they might pray and be caught out by heaven. Rather than do that, they have a little black thing on the back of the head which stays there permanently, even when they take their hat off. That has no foundation either. It is another thing that is a false conception.

First Century Customs

We are told the veil had to do with married women and that it corresponded to the wedding ring. Therefore, if you have a wedding ring, you can remove your hat. For the spinsters, this is rather sad; but for the married ladies, you can remove your hat because your wedding ring is your covering. This is fallacious! Maybe in certain quarters there was such a thing, but never in Jewish circles. In fact, it was the unmarried girls that always wore the veil, and the married ones who could more easily discard it. They never did discard it. It is quite the other way. This is a theory of adjustment, and we have got to be very careful. There is no ground for it. It is not even a weak fact; it is a false fact.

Then, the false conception which I was brought up on was that, in Corinth, the loose women of the streets never wore a veil. The apostle was so afraid that the Christian ladies would be thought of as women of the street that he said all this. In other words, it is only to do with the first century; it has nothing to do with us today. This is perfectly true, but does the apostle really mean this to go to such lengths? Why doesn't he simply say, "You know that all around you there are these kind of ladies; you cannot do this kind of thing!" Why does he say, "Because of the angels ..."? The same people who say it belongs to the first century tell us they believed in the first century that angels were present at their worship. So now, we find that a whole passage has absolutely no relevance to any other century than the first two. Where do we end? Shall we throw baptism out? Shall we throw other things out? Where do we end on such a thing?

There are many other things that are said on this matter of first century custom, about it being old-fashioned and antiquarian. We are told that, in those days, the ladies were veiled from head to foot, that you saw absolutely nothing. It is true, of course, that in parts of the world where women, and the position of women, were degraded and devalued, they were so veiled. But it has been one of the glories of Jewish history that never in its history (except when they came from Padan-Aram, which was not really looked upon in quite the same way) did Jewish women ever have their faces veiled. Their heads were veiled, but never their faces. It is a weak or false fact upon which a tremendous amount is built. The whole thing is an argument about ladies being swathed in a black veil from head to foot out of which there were two peepholes. Of course, some people who visited the East saw Bedouin ladies with this black thing all over them, with two little slits, and all sorts of coins, and said, "Now that is what it was like in the old days when the Apostle Paul wrote the letter to the Corinthians." It is absolute nonsense!

A Sign of Spirituality

I wish I could believe that spirituality could be so quickly acquired. The tragedy of it, for some of us who rebelled against this whole matter when we were younger, is that it was thought the older the hat and the more dowdy the appearance, the more spiritual the sister. I remember, when we were young, sitting behind some sisters in certain conferences, wanting to push back the pins in their bun. It was sticking out all over, a kind of unkempt, careless attitude; and this was supposed to be spirituality. No wonder people have reacted against something like that. That is entirely false. Putting a hat on no more makes a person spiritual than does anything else outward.

A Sign That the Church Is a Man's World

This is wickedly untrue. The sisters do not have to speak to have a very great influence in the church. Sometimes, when sisters speak too much, they lose their influence. God has so positioned us, so constituted us, as men and women, that women can influence things very, very greatly by just being quiet and just being women. The old saying is, "Behind every man stands a great woman." Sisters have a tremendous influence; and it is only when women are insecure that they have to throw their weight around, they have to tell people to do this and that. They have to jump in and tell people when they are wrong.

The Hat Is Only to Be Worn at The Lord's Table

I was always amazed, in some of the places I went to, none of the sisters wore a hat at all; but suddenly, at the Lord's table, from the depths of portmanteau and trunks, wicker hats appeared. Everyone came with a hat. I have seen this often when we have been on holiday and elsewhere. The people seem to think the Lord's table is the meeting of the church, so you wear a hat for that; but at other gatherings, you can choose. Then again, if you move into a house for a church gathering, you don't have to wear a thing. This just reveals our conception of the church. And there is a variation of this idea that you only have to wear something on your head when you pray or prophesy. I call that a misconception.

The Testimony of Brothers

In what way are sisters a sign in the church to this matter of covering? Perhaps we will begin to see this matter more clearly if we first take a look at the brothers. The whole problem is that everyone thinks that the woman is the sign. But, if we look at the brothers first to see what they signify, we shall see much more clearly what the sisters' significance or testimony is. The man represents Christ as the image of God.

> For a man indeed ought not to have his head veiled,
> forasmuch as he is the image and glory of God: but the
> woman is the glory of the man. 1 Corinthians 11:7

> A man ought not to cover his head for he represents
> the very person and glory of God. J. B. Phillips

The fact of the man's head being uncovered was the sensational thing in Paul's day. I do wish everyone could get hold of this. There was absolutely no question about women having their heads covered; they had always had their heads covered. But the fact was, up to that point, men had their heads covered as well. They had the prayer shawl. No child of God, under the Old Covenant, would ever come before God without drawing the prayer shawl over his head. Most of them wore something on their heads, especially the Pharisee, all the time. When the priests went into the presence of the Lord, they never took those hats off. They had to be carefully clothed with special hats, headwear. What did it all mean?

It was sensational when the early Christian men uncovered their heads and stood before God, praying and worshiping and contributing in the gatherings of the people, without something on their heads. It was only in pagan worship that they ever uncovered their heads in that way. The prayer shawl or the hat was a sign that there was a veil between God and man; something blocked heaven. The heaven above the man and the woman's head was closed. The covering on the head was a sign of that. But, he is to pray or prophesy with his head uncovered. The veil is gone, torn in two. Heaven is opened above him. Sin has been dealt with by Christ. He is the only one who inherently had an open heaven. Remember when heaven opened at His baptism? "This is my beloved Son in whom I am well pleased" (Matthew 3:17). Heaven had never opened to a human being before, but it opened to the Lord Jesus Christ. The man is a sign of the Lord Jesus Christ, upon Whom there is an open heaven, Who has dealt with our sin and torn away the veil. In the early days of the church, that was sensational. It was so sensational that the sisters said: "Aren't we included? This is so marvelous; this is so absolutely wonderful to see all the brothers standing there without anything on their heads. It thrills us. Why can't we throw off the veil as well? We are all one; we are all saved."

This is the whole point of why the apostle had to write to them and say: "Don't do it, don't do it. The men signify something and you sisters signify something else. If you disregard this difference, you will lose something very, very precious. The woman represents the church, not Christ. She represents the church as the glory of Christ." It says in this passage: " ... the woman is the glory of the man." The woman represents the church as the glory of Christ; "His fulness, who filleth all in all." The men have the privilege of reminding all of us, brothers and sisters, that Christ has an open heaven–the veil is gone. And the sisters have this wonderful privilege of saying before us all: "We are the church. In ourselves we have no open heaven, but we have an open heaven in Christ." So don't let any of us who are saved think: "We are something in ourselves. Heaven opened to us because of what we are." We often think that having been saved by His grace, we can persuade God to bless us through our good works. No! The sister is the perpetual reminder that the only way the church has communication with heaven is through her Head, through the Lord Jesus. She is taken out of Him. Her place is to be together with Him, to be part of Him, to be His complement.

Eve Taken Out of Adam

This is why the passage we read in Genesis 2 is fundamental to this whole matter; and also why the passage we read in Ephesians 5 throws so much light on this whole thing. Why did God do this with Adam? It begins in Genesis 2 with this comment: "And there was found no help meet for him." Immediately afterwards, God produced all the animals of the field, brought them all before Adam and said, "Adam, would you name these creatures?" I used to think, when I was first saved, that was the strangest way of doing things. Why didn't God name them since He had created them? "We will call this a rhinoceros, and we will call this an orangutan, and we will call this a giraffe", and so on. But no, it was man who had to do it. What was God doing? He was trying to make Adam realize that he was not complete, that it was only half of him there. Actually, the other part was in him, and God had to get it out. So, He put him to sleep.

There wasn't a single one of those creatures that Adam could live with. He looked at them all and named them, and they trotted off or loped off. But there wasn't a single one, not even the orangutan (that I am told is supposed to be man's great ancestor) that he felt, "Well now, there is nothing else; perhaps I will settle down with her." But never! So God put him to sleep, opened his side, took out bone and fashioned woman. Woman was a creation of God just as man was. Then He woke Adam and said, "Here." Now Adam didn't say, "Oh, this is such-and-such; we will call it such-and-such." He said, "This is entirely different; this is bone of my bone, and flesh of my flesh. I can feel it. This is my other half. I will call her woman because she has been taken out of man." The two belonged to each other.

This is a picture of what God did with our Lord Jesus. Do you remember that extraordinary statement of John, the apostle, when he told of the soldier who stood by the Lord Jesus when He died, when He fell asleep? The soldier ran the spear into His side and forthwith there came out blood and water, and John made so much of it. He said: "I, who stood by, bear witness to this, and my witness is true." Then he emphasized it again. He was trying to tell us that that blood and water has produced something out of the open side of the dead Christ. People say, "Oh, but it is redemption." Yes, of course; but the redemption was already ours; there was no need to open His side. The opening of His side was to make us to understand what God did with Adam when He took Eve out of her. Through the blood and through the water, God has taken an elect people for Himself. When the Lord Jesus was raised from the dead, it was just as if God was presenting a church to Him. And He said: "This is bone of my bone and flesh of my flesh. She shall be called the church, because she has been taken out of me." When you understand that, you begin to understand the whole matter of covering.

I remember a dear brother, in almost the last message he ever gave, saying that Eve was taken out of Adam, and there was a sense in which he always felt that the only place of security and safety for her was when she pressed back into his side. While she was pressed into his side, she was secure and safe. She was covered.

The Church's Safety in Christ

Some of the sisters say, "Why should we have to do that?" But the fact of the matter is, it is a picture of the church. Do you think the Lord Jesus has to flee to the church for security and safety? Think of it like that. Do you think He has to appeal to us to enclose and protect Him, to keep Him? Of course not! When we see it in spiritual terms, immediately the whole thing falls into place. We begin to see that the place of the church is to be hid with Christ, to be concealed by Him, to be hedged in by Him, to be enclosed by Him, to be protected by Him, to be overlaid.

It is not just by the woman's head covering, but in her very constitution, her very behavior, her very outlook, her very attitude and also her dress, that she is to be the sign in the church of this tremendous truth. She is to remind all the brothers, as well as the sisters, that the only safety we have is to be pressed into the side of Christ.

Oh Lamb of God still keep me, close to Thy wounded side. Tis only there in safety and peace, I can abide.

Some people seem to think this matter of wearing a hat or something on the head is just something for sisters to remind them all to be subject, to shut up; but, it is not that. It is far, far greater than that. Do you think that the angels are so bothered? No, there is something far greater than that. The significance of the woman's dress and of her behavior, of the fact that she is a sign, is to remind the whole church that their only safety is in Christ; they have come out of Christ and their safety is in Him. The woman's testimony is this: only IN CHRIST is there an open heaven; only IN HIM is there no more veil; only in dependence ON HIM is there safety. Outside of Him—destruction.

What Head Covering Signifies

The Supremacy and Centrality of Christ

For a man indeed ought not to have his head veiled, forasmuch as he is the image and glory of God: but the woman is the glory of the man. For the man is not of the woman; but the woman of the man: for neither was the man created for the woman; but the woman for the man. 1 Corinthians 11:7–9

Translate this immediately, in the light of Genesis 2 and Ephesians 5, into spiritual terms, and you have it. Christ was not created for us; we were created for Him. We came out of Him and have been created for Him; and we are His glory. So the sister is a testimony to the supremacy and centrality of the Lord Jesus Christ. In a sense, she reminds all of us, brothers as well, that the Lord Jesus is everything. We have come out of Him. That is our origin, our source. The source of our salvation, the source of our life, the source of our well-being and the source of our fulfillment is Him. We have been created for Him, to please Him, to satisfy Him and to be a joy to Him. We are His glory. It is all understood when we see it as Christ and the church; and this is exactly what Ephesians 5 tries to tell us. It states quite clearly that this whole matter is something much more than husbands and wives or man and woman; it is the church. The church is to be subject to Christ. The wives' subjection to their husbands is a picture of something. We get such unhappy ideas about subjection, as if it is servility; as if it means that there is no possibility of communication, no possibility of expression and no possibility of mutual fellowship. Oh, the ideas, the bitterness, that have come into this matter! It is so tragic.

We know that the church is Christ's inheritance. It is spoken of as "His inheritance in the saints in light". That is why we have to emphasize so much this tremendous matter of the building of the church because it is His inheritance; it is His bride. When you think of it like that, you begin to understand the significance of this testimony to Christ as being everything. The church looks upon Him "as all and in all". Remember, then, what covering means: to conceal, to hedge in, to enclose, to protect, to overlay.

"In Christ": concealed in Him, enclosed in Him, hedged in by Him, protected by Him, covered by Him, overlaid by Him, abiding in Him. There is the testimony. Every time the sister takes her place in the gathering of the church, she ought to be a shining sign to this thing: "All of you are in Christ. There is no dowdiness here, no crumpled old hats here. There is something wonderful about this. It is glorious; it is absolutely marvelous. Look everyone; I don't have to say a single word; I am preaching a sermon by my presence here. I am to you all an encouragement and a warning."

The Mediatorship of Christ

The woman's head covered signifies that there is no open heaven except in Christ and through Christ. Again, there is something marvelous in this testimony. She is reminding us continually of this one thing.

> *Jesus saith unto him, I am the way, and the truth, and the life: no one cometh unto the Father, but by me. John 14:6*

Did you know, sisters, that you are a testimony to that? When you put something on your head, you are simply saying: there is no open heaven except through HIM; the veil is not rent except through HIM; there is no way except through HIM; there is no truth except through HIM; there is no reality except through HIM; there is no life except through HIM; there is no experience except through HIM; there is no way to the Father except through HIM.

When you begin to understand this wonderful Scripture, "For there is one mediator between God and men, himself man, Christ Jesus, who gave himself a ransom for all" (1 Timothy 3:5–6). Then you know that this testimony is something that the angels are very interested in. When they see it disregarded, and despised, there is a shock: "How can that be, that those folks there just disregard this? Of course, the motive is right; but why do they disregard it? Why don't they at least inquire?" There is shock in heaven if the kind of testimony we don't even realize we are bearing is saying: "Christ is not supreme, He is not central and He is not all. We have an open heaven in ourselves; we have a right to it." If a sister were to think, "We are speaking for ourselves as sisters; the brothers have a right to an open heaven, but not we sisters", this is nonsense. They are speaking for the whole and saying, "There is no way through except this."

In Christ there is absolute safety, absolute security, absolute provision, absolute victory and absolute fulfillment. This is what the testimony of this mediatorship really means. It is not just that Christ stands between us and God. That is one tremendous cornerstone; but it is more than that. He is the means by which we are fulfilled; the means by which the will of God and purpose of God are fulfilled and realized in our lives; the means by which, through the Holy Spirit, all the fulness of God comes to us and we are complete in Him. What a wonderful privilege to remind everyone, every time: "Look here, everyone; I don't have to say a word. I am preaching a sermon. I am declaring something through my very presence here.

Outside of Him, there is nothing but harm, danger and destruction. You would immediately see that there is no way of getting to God except through Jesus Christ. Do you not know that? But how slowly we learn it. People are trying to get fulness of the Spirit; they are trying to get holiness; they are trying to get this and trying to get that apart from Christ, as if it is an experience in itself. But this testimony is virtually saying that is impossible. Only harm, counterfeit and superficial experience can come that way.

The Headship of Christ

But I would have you know, that the head of every man is Christ; and the head of the woman is the man; and the head of Christ is God. 1 Corinthians 11:3

For the husband is the head of the wife, as Christ also is the head of the church, being himself the saviour of the body. Ephesians 5:23

The authority of Christ, the Name of Christ and the relationship to Him is what is testified to in this matter. When a woman marries a man, she takes his name; and when you and I were saved, God gave us the Name of Jesus. We were named with the Name of Jesus Christ so that we can pray in His Name; we can gather in His Name; and whatsoever we do, we do in His Name. It is not that we tack it on the end all the time. That could be an empty little epithet. Some people use the Name of Jesus as if it is just a charm, and then cannot understand why something does not happen. But it is the inward truth behind the use of that Name which is the thing that matters. When you pray in the Name of

Jesus, what are you saying? You are saying: "I am in Him, Father. I am married to Him; I belong to Him; I am one with Him."

The sister is to remind us of the headship of Jesus Christ, the authority of Christ and our relationship to Him. She is to remind us all that there is only one Lord, one mind, one will and one way in the church. She is simply to remind us that we don't do what other people think, but only what the Head says. Covering is being obedient to the Lord; uncovering is getting out of His will.

Divine Order and Distinctions

But I would have you know, that the head of every man is Christ; and the head of the woman is the man; and the head of Christ is God. Every man praying or prophesying, having his head covered, dishonoreth his head. But every woman praying or prophesying with her head unveiled dishonoreth her head; for it is one and the same thing as if she were shaven. 1 Corinthians 11:3–5

There is a distinction made between men and women. It has nothing to do with inequality or inferiority but it has all to do with the difference of function and of gift. God has made men and women different, and we live in days when that difference is being obscured. We live in days of what is called unisex. You cannot imagine anything more diametrically opposed and contradictory to the mind of God. Nature itself teaches us that men and women are different. So why try to abolish the difference? We have been constituted physically different, we have been constituted mentally different and we are complementary to each other.

The whole question of divine order and distinction is simply this: God has placed us in a different way; men and women, husbands and wives, and so on. There is difference in function and there is difference in gift. In one sense, you could say there is difference in position; but there is absolute equality.

There can be neither Jew nor Greek, there can be neither bond nor free, there can be no male and female; for ye all are one man in Christ Jesus. Galatians 3:28

There is the absolute equality of every saved soul: "neither male nor female". But we are still male and female; and as such, we have an essential part to play in the church. This is something that all of us have to ask the Lord to help us over; because we are living in days when the whole pressure of society and its teaching is to destroy the distinctions in the home and in every other part of society. They can not be disregarded.

What is this testimony about divine order? I know of no subject over which people can get so easily uncovered as the matter of divine order. It is the easiest thing in the world to disregard divine order, to contradict divine order. When we come up against flesh and blood, we get our eyes so filled with the flesh and blood that it is the easiest thing in the world to lash out at them, and then to find out afterwards that we have come right up against divine order. We have come into collision with something which is divinely ordained and appointed of God. Therefore, God takes it up. When that happens, there is uncovering.

We went through the Old Testament, seeing example after example of this very kind of thing, the setting aside of divine order. We read of Korah, Dothan, Abiram, Miriam, Aaron and case after case, given to us as examples of this very thing, for our instruction, upon whom the end of the ages have come. It is so easy to do it. We can do it in the home. We can do it at work. We can do it in society; "for the magistrate is as God to us", as the Scripture says. Remember when the Apostle Paul said to the magistrate, who happened to be the high priest, "... whited wall, tottering wall"? The guard who stood by struck him on the face and said, "Do you dare to speak to the high priest, the magistrate, like that?" And when the apostle, (who had bad sight) recognized him, he said: "I am very sorry; I didn't realize it was he." The fact was that the high priest was a tottering wall; but he had contradicted divine order, and he apologized for it.

This question is so tremendously important I do not know how to cover it except to say that it goes far deeper than just a question of position in the church. In 1 Corinthians 12, we are told there is diversity in unity. It is not a question of inequality; it is a question of diversity. This one is this, this one is that, the other is this. God has set some in the church this, that, and the other. This whole matter of the wearing of something on the head is a testimony to divine order. It is not in itself so important, as if God wants His people to wear something on the head, as if He wants two-thirds of those who make up the church to always be permanently covered. There is something deeper; the sisters remind us of divine order in all things.

The Mystery of Covering

For this cause ought the woman to have a sign of authority
on her head, because of the angels. 1 Corinthians 11:10

If for no other reason, we ought to stop and reflect deeply on
this phrase, " ... because of the angels". Is it not an evidence that
there is no fear of God in us, if we can chuck overboard a whole
passage with something like that in the midst of it? I would have
thought that one phrase would have halted even the most fearless,
at least to make them think again. This whole matter has much
more in it than something physical or even something only to do
with things visible. It somehow affects the angels. How does it
affect the angels? I can only say that the whole subject is lifted,
by this phrase, on to another level, something of which we need
to take a more serious note. We touch the mystery of covering–
the whole mystery of it. Somehow, it affects the unseen world,
the unseen host, fallen and unfallen. It affects principalities and
powers because it is not just merely to do with people wearing
something on the head; it is the significance of it; it is what that
action signifies.

We ought also to note two things mentioned in 1 Corinthians
11:2–16, which are often confused. On the one hand, we have the
hair also called the woman's glory (v.15), and secondly, we have the
veil or covering, also called authority on the head (v.10). These two
things are often confused because of the statement of the apostle
in verse 15 that the hair is her covering. Now, another Greek word
altogether is used there in that connection. This is what I mean
by weak or false facts. People read the Authorized Version, which

used the same word covering all the way through, and then they say: "Oh well, now it is quite clear. I don't quite understand it, but it seems that the hair is the covering." But it does not say that. Professor Bruce, in his paraphrase, inserts the word: "The hair is her natural covering." The apostle's argument is: because the hair is the natural covering, it needs to be covered. Now you think, "That is a very strange and almost irrational argument, isn't it?" He goes on to say that if she does not have something on the head, let her cut off all her hair. Therefore, the thing he is arguing for is that if she has got long hair, let her wear something on it. Do you remember the Scripture we read in Isaiah 4:5, "Over all the glory a covering"? It is mystery; and I cannot explain it. I only know that the hair of the woman is called her glory, and the authority on the head (the word sign is not there) is that there is something covering it. There is a token as a covering, something that signifies.

We are touching divine and eternal mystery, and this is what the sister reminds us of: there is something here beyond us. We believers have been introduced into a sphere which we don't fully comprehend or understand. In Christ, we are safe; we are covered in Him. But beware that we are all really abiding in Him. That is really the significance of it. It is the sister's privilege, by her presence, by her attitude, by her dress, to remind all of us concerning this vitally important matter of covering. She is an encouragement to the whole church, an exhortation to the whole church, a comfort to the whole church, to every one of us to take his or her position in Christ and praise the Lord, come before the Lord, and intercede before the Lord. On the other hand, she is a solemn warning and reminder of the danger of being uncovered or getting uncovered.

When most people come into a Christian gathering they bow their heads. What do you say? It is so empty in some cases that I have known people who said: "Lord, for what we are about to receive, make us truly grateful." It is because they are not thinking. Next time you see a sister there with something upon her head, bow your head and say: "Lord, I take my place in Christ. Here I am in Him, clothed with the garments of salvation."

I trust that all the sisters will be lifted so entirely out of bondage in this matter that their faces will shine under those hats and so help everyone to really rejoice in the Lord. There is nothing more terrible than this awful bondage and rebellion.

What is the point of wearing a hat if it is something like that? I do not wish to be cheap, but what would you think of the Lord's table if the bread was moldy? You would be shocked. You would think, "We know it is a sign and there is not much in the sign itself; but shouldn't we all be careful?" That goes for the brothers, too. How we need to be careful so that we really are a testimony to the Lord. There is something very wonderful in this whole matter. Only God can throw more light upon it because a study like this can create as many problems as it seeks to solve. But by opening up the whole matter, and with our openness of heart and spirit, and the Word of God and the Holy Spirit as our guide and teacher, we can search out the Scriptures, whether these things be so. The Lord help us all, above everything else, to be covered; not just physically covered, but truly, inwardly covered, by abiding in HIM.

Shall we pray:

Our Father, we need divine enlightenment. It is so easy to do something because someone says it ought to be done or because we feel that everyone else does it. But our prayer, beloved Lord, is that there may come to us divine enlightenment, and we may begin to understand that there is more in this whole matter than perhaps we ever realized. Oh Lord, tackle anything that is just rebellious, or dark, or bound, or dead. Grant, we pray that the glorious privilege of being, in any way, a testimony may come to each one of us. We pray for the sisters, Lord, that they may truly be a testimony; and we pray for the brothers, that they also may be a true testimony. Help us, then, in this matter, we pray. We ask it together in the name of our Lord Jesus Christ. Amen.

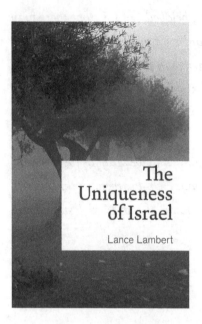

The Uniqueness of Israel

Woven into the fabric of Jewish existence there is an undeniable uniqueness. There is bitter controversy over the subject of Israel, but time itself will establish the truth about this nation's place in God's plan. For Lance Lambert, the Lord Jesus is the key that unlocks Jewish history He is the key not only to their fall, but also to their restoration. For in spite of the fact that they rejected Him, He has not rejected them.

Till the Day Dawns

"And we have the word of prophecy made more sure; whereunto ye do well that ye take heed, as unto a lamp shining in a dark place, until the day dawn, and the day-star arise in your hearts." (II Peter 1:9).

The word of prophecy was not given that we might merely be comforted but that we would be prepared and made ready. Let us look into the Word of God together, searching out the prophecies, that the Day-Star arise in our hearts until the Day dawns.

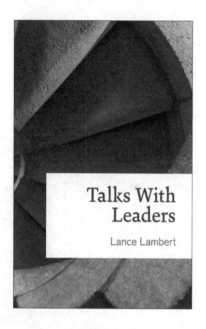

Talks With Leaders

"O Timothy, guard that which is committed unto thee ..." (I Timothy 6:20) Has God given you something? Has God deposited something in you? Is there something of Himself which He has given to you to contribute to the people of God? Guard it. Guard that vision which He has given you. Guard that understanding that He has so mercifully granted to you. Guard that experience which He has given that it does not evaporate or drain away or become a cause of pride. Guard that which the Lord has given to you by the Holy Spirit. In these heart-to-heart talks with leaders Lance Lambert covers such topics as the character of God's servants, the way to serve, the importance of anointing, and hearing God's voice. Let us consider together how to remain faithful with what has been entrusted to us.

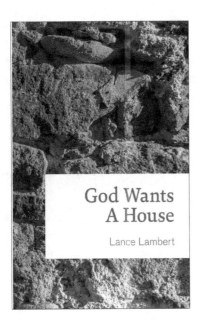

God Wants a House

Where is God at home? Is He at home in Richmond, VA? Is He at home in Washington? Is He at home in Richmond, Surrey? Is He at home in these other places? Where is God at home? There are thousands of living stones, many, many dear believers with real experience of the Lord, but where has the ark come home? Where are the staves being lengthened that God has finally come home? In God Wants a House Lance looks into this desire of the Lord, this desire He has to dwell with His people. What would this dwelling look like? Let's seek the Lord, that we can say with David, "One thing have I asked of Jehovah, that will I seek after: that I may dwell in the house of Jehovah all the days of my life, To behold the beauty of Jehovah, And to inquire in his temple."